WOOD PROJECTS FOR THE GARDEN

Created and designed by the editorial staff of ORTHO BOOKS

Editor
Kate Rider

Writers
Ron Hildebrand
Gene and Katie Hamilton

Illustrator
Ron Hildebrand

Ortho Books

Publisher
Robert J. Dolezal

Production Director
Ernie S. Tasaki

Managing Editors
Karin Shakery
Michael D. Smith
Sally W. Smith

System Manager
Leonard D. Grotta

National Sales Manager
Charles H. Aydelotte

Marketing Specialist
Susan B. Boyle

Operations Coordinator
Georgiann Wright

Administrative Assistant
Deborah Tibbetts

Senior Technical Analyst
J. A. Crozier, Jr.

Chevron Chemical Company
6001 Bollinger Canyon Road, San Ramon, CA 94583

▬▬▬▬▬▬▬
Acknowledgments

Consultants
Craig A. Bergquist
Chris E. Hecht

Copy Chief
Melinda Levine

Copyeditor
Judith Dunham

Composition and Pagination
Linda M. Bouchard
Robert C. Miller

Proofreader
Andrea Y. Connolly

Indexer
Elinor Lindheimer

Editorial Assistants
Teri Lammers
Leslie Tilley

Production by
Studio 165

Photographs by
Ortho photo library
Laurie Black, front cover, pages 48, 76, 80, 86, 88

Photographic Stylist
Sara Slavin, front cover, pages 48, 76, 80, 86, 88

Illustration Assistants
Frank Hildebrand
Judith Spratt

Project Design and Construction
Clyde Childress, page 20
R. J. DeCristoforo, pages 27, 34, 36, 53–58, 64, 68, 69, 72–75, 84, 90–92
L. Fabri, page 18
Gene and Katie Hamilton, pages 32, 33, 88 (design)
Ron Hildebrand, page 22
Michael Landis, pages 12, 13, 16, 17, 24, 28, 30, 38, 40, 42, 46, 60, 62, 66, 71, 82
Peter S. Malakoff, Mitch Berman, pages 48, 76, 78, 80, 86, 88 (construction)
J. Matthias, page 19
Richard Ray, pages 14, 52, 70

Special Thanks to
Linda Bouchard
Charlene Droheim, California Redwood Association
Dr. and Mrs. Robert Greene
Smith & Hawken, Mill Valley, Calif.
Michael Landis
Tamara Mallory
Cindy Putnam

Separations by
Color Tech Corporation

Lithographed in USA by
Webcrafters, Inc.

Front cover. The elegant Garden Swing is designed to be durable as well as attractive. For more information and instructions for building this project, see page 86.

Page 1. The Umbrella Table and its set of matching chairs make a handsome and useful addition to any patio or deck. See page 76.

Page 3. The Sunburst Trellis, with its accompanying planter boxes, provides a decorative support for plants. Instructions are on page 50.

Back cover:
Upper left. This large, handsomely designed picnic table and matching benches encourage outdoor meals and activities. See page 80.

Upper right. Covered with a flowering vine, the Dowel Trellis adds a burst of color to a wall or fence. This project is one of the simplest trellises to construct. See page 34.

Lower left. These portable A-frame Shelves are handy for displaying a collection of potted plants. Instructions are on page 92.

Lower right. The Layered Planter is simple to make, and can be filled with soil for planting or used to hide a large pot. See page 21.

WOOD PROJECTS FOR THE GARDEN

WOOD IN THE GARDEN

Constructing wood projects for your yard and garden offers many rewards besides just the fun of building them. Many of the projects in this book will help bring your family outdoors, make garden chores easier, expand the uses of your yard, and enhance the style and ambiance of your home. Building projects yourself allows you to tailor them to your own specific needs and tastes.

In this book you'll find a wide variety of projects, from planter boxes and trellises to swings and umbrella-shaded picnic tables. Some are practical gardening aids; others are decorative, finished pieces to display on a deck or patio; and others are space savers to help organize a small garden. Step-by-step instructions guide you through the construction of each project, and color illustrations and photographs show details. Materials lists help you compose your lumberyard shopping list.

The book is divided into five sections, enabling you to easily locate the type of project you are looking for. Within each section the projects usually appear in order of increasing complexity, but it's not necessary to build one project before going on to another—skip around and make those that appeal to you. An introductory section explains what you'll need to know about lumber, tools, and woodworking techniques.

We hope you will enjoy building these projects, and that you will see them as a starting point for more additions to your garden. Customize the projects for your own needs, and let them set your imagination going. The ways you can use wood in the garden are almost unlimited.

A trellis, planter box, and raised bed made of wood blend into this garden and deck. These are just a few of the many types of projects you can build to enhance your own home and garden.

GETTING STARTED

Outdoor projects require different types of wood, hardware, and glue than those used in other types of construction. This section tells how to select and finish wood for outdoor use, describes the hardware and tools used in the projects, and provides tips on working with tools.

Wood for Outdoor Projects

In choosing lumber, you'll have to consider many factors, including cost, availability, the use and desired appearance of your project, and the special requirements for wood that will be used outdoors. The information on the following pages will help you know what to look for when buying lumber for outdoor projects.

Be very selective when shopping for lumber, especially with lower-grade lumber. Take time to appraise each piece, looking for warped boards and defects. Higher grades are more costly, but buying the best grade you can afford is worthwhile.

Suitable types of wood. All of the projects in this book call for softwood, which comes from coniferous trees. Softwoods—including redwood, pine, fir, and cypress—are generally less expensive than hardwoods and are more practical for projects that will be used outdoors.

Redwood is called for in most of the projects, but you can use other types of wood that are more readily available in your area or would be better for your specific needs. Just make sure that the wood you choose is suitable for outdoor use, and that its particular properties fit the project. For instance, cedar is not a good

material for benches and decks because it splinters easily.

Most wood is subject to decay and insect attack and is therefore unsuitable for outdoor use. For projects that will be in contact with the ground or will be exposed to cycles of wet and dry weather, it is important to use lumber that is naturally decay resistant, such as the heartwood of redwood, cedar, and cypress. Another possibility for outdoor projects is pressure-treated lumber, which is described below.

Lumber sizes. Softwoods are usually available in standard thicknesses and widths, in lengths starting at 8 feet and going to 20 feet in 2-foot increments. Thickness and width are always specified in nominal dimensions: the size of the board when first sawed at the mill. The actual size of surfaced wood is smaller because a certain amount of material is removed during surfacing. Thus, a surfaced 1 by 2 measures approximately ¾ inch by 1½ inches. Generally, the thickness of 1-inch stock is reduced by ¼

inch, 2-inch stock by ½ inch. Widths are reduced by ½ inch in boards up to 6 inches wide, and by ¾ inch thereafter. The actual size of rough-cut lumber, on the other hand, is the same as the nominal dimensions; a rough-cut 2 by 4, for example, measures 2 inches by 4 inches.

It is best not to order pieces that must be cut to a nonstandard length. If you need a number of 5-foot pieces, order 10-foot stock and cut it to length yourself.

The choice of rough or surfaced lumber is determined by the final use of the project. For furniture, surfaced wood is called for. For raised beds and other less finished projects—where splinters and a rough surface will not pose a problem—rough lumber is used.

Wood seasoning. Seasoning is a process that reduces the natural moisture content of green wood. Seasoned lumber may be either air-dried or kiln-dried. Air-drying reduces the moisture content of wood to 14 to 18 percent. Kiln-dried lumber has no

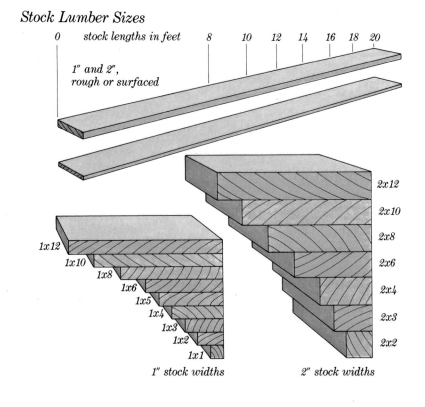

Stock Lumber Sizes

0   stock lengths in feet   8   10   12   14   16   18   20

1" and 2", rough or surfaced

2x12
2x10
2x8
2x6
2x4
2x3
2x2

1x12
1x10
1x8
1x6
1x5
1x4
1x3
1x2
1x1

1" stock widths   2" stock widths

more than 6 to 9 percent moisture content. The higher the moisture content, the more the wood will tend to shrink and warp with time. Drier wood is stronger and more stable than green wood, but it is also more costly. Air-dried lumber is suitable for general construction, but you may want to use kiln-dried wood for benches, tables, and similar projects where appearance and precise joints are important.

Surfaced, green lumber is stamped S-GRN and will probably twist, shrink, and warp as it dries. Dry lumber is stamped either S-DRY for surfaced-dry or MC-15 for moisture content 15 percent.

Pressure-treating. Pressure-treated lumber, which has preservatives permanently locked into it, is far superior to wood that has been merely sprayed or dipped in a chemical preservative. Slightly green or beige in color, it does not darken if left to weather.

When buying treated lumber, specify whether it is for ground contact or use aboveground so the salesperson can recommend the proper material. Also indicate whether or not you plan to paint or stain the wood; some types of preservatives are more difficult to paint over than others.

Pressure-treated wood should only be used for projects where it will not be in contact with food, skin, or clothing, however, since it is toxic. Manufacturers of pressure-treated lumber issue a "Consumer Information Sheet" and distribute it where pressure-treated wood is sold. Read this sheet so you are aware of the toxic nature of the treating chemicals and the guidelines for the safe use of treated lumber recommended by the manufacturer and the Environmental Protection Agency.

Wood quality. In addition to the decay-resistant properties of wood, its overall quality is also important. All lumber is graded at the mill according to exacting national standards, and these grades are good indicators of the strength, appearance, and durability of wood. See the softwood

grading chart below for an explanation of the grades.

Plywood. Plywood is a practical garden-project material, but it must be exterior-grade to be used on outdoor projects. It is available in thicknesses from ¼ to ¾ inch and in sheets measuring 4 by 8 feet. It is a good idea to seal all exposed ply-

wood edges to prevent water from penetrating and causing layers to come apart. This can be done with a suitable water repellent and decay retardant, or with a paint product, or even with a coat of waterproof glue.

Panels of house siding make an attractive material for garden projects, but some are treated with

Softwood Grades (including special names for grades of redwood)

Examples of domestic softwoods: western white pine, redwood, Engelmann spruce, Sitka spruce, western larch, ponderosa pine, shortleaf pine, sugar pine, white fir, bald cypress, incense cedar, western red cedar.

Classification	Grade	Description
Select	A	practically flawless; excellent choice for stains and natural finishes
	B	similar to A grade, but may contain a limited number of small defects—usable for stains and natural finishes
	C	defects that can be concealed with paint are permitted
	D	also usable for paint finishes, but will contain more defects than C grade
Common	#1	a good utility lumber that may contain some blemishes and tight knots—standards say it should be free of warpage, checks, splits, and decay
	#2	fairly sound wood, but may have checks, loose knots, and discoloration—no splits or warpage
	#3	medium-quality construction lumber; all types of defects are permitted; some bad sections may have to be cut out
	#4	low-quality construction lumber; may contain numerous defects of all types; open knot holes permitted
	#5	lowest quality wood, used mostly as a filler; considerable amounts of waste often encountered
Structural*	Construction	the highest quality structural material
	Standard	similar in quality to construction grade, but with slight defects permitted
	Utility	poor structural qualities; often used where additional members contribute more strength
	Economy	lowest quality structural material
Redwood	Clear all heart	top quality; one face completely free of defects, opposite face may have no more than two pin knots regardless of board size; excellent stability; usually kiln-dried
	Clear	high-quality finish lumber similar to clear all heart, but may contain sapwood, some small knots, and medium surface checks; usually kiln-dried
	Select heart	all sound heartwood; available in surfaced or unsurfaced condition; usually not kiln-dried; knots permitted
	Construction heart**	an economical all-purpose grade; good choice for posts, decks, and smaller garden projects; usually not kiln-dried
	Select	very similar to select heart, but used where termites and decay are not problems
	Construction common**	a good all-purpose material, but for above-grade construction; contains sapwood; knots permitted
	Merchantable**	contains larger and looser knots and more imperfections than other grades; heartwood and sapwood are included in this grade, so some pieces are good for ground-contact projects

*structural lumber is graded mainly for strength
**often designated as garden grades

water repellents and decay retardants that contain toxic chemicals. When using these panels for a container or similar project, it's wise to line the interior with polyurethane plastic or to coat it with a liquid asphalt or a material such as pruning paint.

Cutting Wood to Size

In general, when working on the projects in this book, it is best to cut the pieces as you go along instead of cutting them all at the start. This is because the thickness and width of lumber can vary, and you may find that you need to compensate for these discrepancies by making pieces slightly larger or smaller than indicated on the Materials List. For instance, do not cut the base of a planter box to size until you have assembled the sides and ends, and can measure the exact dimensions required for the base. If you measure and cut each piece of wood only when you are ready to attach it, the joints in your project will fit together more precisely.

Finally, although the lengths of all pieces for each project are indicated, feel free to vary the dimensions as necessary to fit your needs, or to use these plans as starting points for your own custom-designed projects.

Wood Protection and Finishing

Any unprotected wood will undergo changes in color, texture, and usually shape when exposed to the weather. Some types of wood finishes will both protect your project from weathering and preserve the natural appearance of the wood. Others can be used to alter the appearance of the wood by adding color or texture.

The type of finish required for a project depends on many factors, including the kind of wood used, the intended use of the project, and the desired appearance.

As mentioned earlier, the heartwood of redwood, cedar, and cypress is naturally decay resistant and does not have to be coated with a finish, but will last longer and look new longer if it is coated. Other types of

wood should be protected with a sealer or approved preservative.

Also consider the use of the project. Tables should be finished so food won't leave a stain and glued joints will stay dry; duckboards covering muddy areas should be coated with a preservative; any project that will be in contact with the ground will last longer if it is protected with a finish. On the other hand, sawhorses, shelves, and some of the other projects don't need a finish if you want a weathered look.

Types of finishes. Clear sealers and water repellents will delay weathering but not retard it completely, and must be renewed periodically. Use a penetrating sealer that will soak into the wood. To ensure that concealed areas will be as protected as exposed ones, apply sealer to all pieces before assembly. If you prefer to allow some weathering, treat at least the concealed areas at the start—especially on containers.

Preservatives last longer than·sealers and inhibit the growth of mildew. Use approved, nontoxic preservatives, such as those containing copper naphthenate, on any project that will be in contact with plants, skin, or food. Some products contain both a sealer and a preservative.

If you want to change the color of the wood, consider a semitransparent (light-bodied) or solid (full-bodied) stain. Semitransparent stains permit a

controllable color change without concealing the natural grain of the wood. Solid stains obscure the grain and can be used to hide defects. Stains can be mixed with a sealer or approved preservative in equal proportions to provide both color change and protection. Check with a supplier to make sure the products you buy are suitable for mixing.

If you decide on paint, select one specifically designed for exterior use, and remember that the project will have to be repainted periodically.

Whichever finish you decide to use, be sure to check that it is recommended for the type of project you are making, and follow the manufacturer's instructions.

▬ Glue

Use only water-resistant or waterproof glue on outdoor projects. The latter is generally more expensive but should be selected for any project that will be permanently exposed to the weather; for more protected projects, water-resistant glue is fine.

The following types of wood glue are readily available:
☐ Plastic resin glues are ureaformaldehyde adhesives that come in powdered form and before using are mixed with water. They contribute great strength to joints and are highly water resistant.
☐ Resorcinol resin glue is completely

Nails	
Nails	Size
2d	1"
3d	1¼"
4d	1½"
5d	1¾"
6d	2"
7d	2¼"
8d	2½"
9d	2¾"
10d	3"
12d	3¼"
16d	3½"
20d	4"

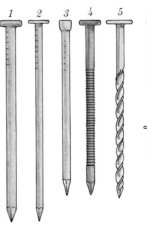

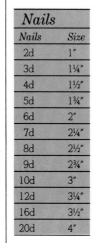

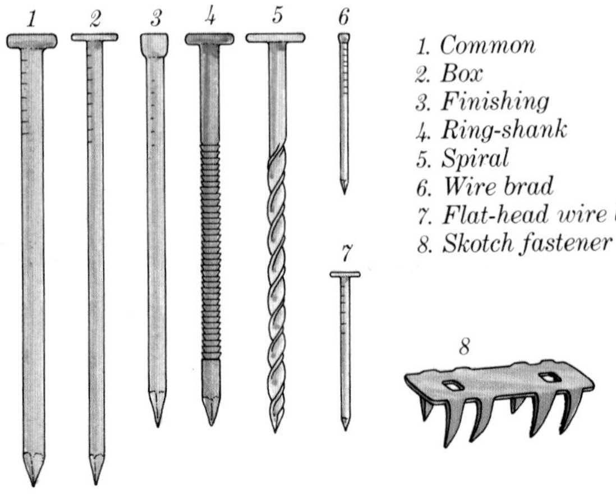

1. Common
2. Box
3. Finishing
4. Ring-shank
5. Spiral
6. Wire brad
7. Flat-head wire brad
8. Skotch fastener

waterproof and comes as a two-component product: a liquid resin and a powdered catalyst. When combined, the two result in an extremely strong adhesive.

☐ Epoxy resins are also two-part, resin-catalyst products. They are waterproof and provide strong adhesive qualities—fine for joining wood to wood and for joining wood to masonry, ceramics, metal, and plastics.

☐ The familiar white glue and yellowish carpenter's wood glue, both widely available in plastic squeeze bottles, are quite strong but are not water resistant. They should be used only on indoor projects. Both these polyvinyl resins are always ready to use. They set up rapidly at room temperature and are colorless so the glue line is invisible.

Application of glue. Before applying any glue, read the instructions on the label. Thoroughly clean mating surfaces and coat them uniformly. When pieces are put together, some glue will squeeze out of the joint. This is fine; just use a sharp knife or chisel to remove the excess after it has dried. Glue left where it isn't meant to be acts like a sealer, preventing even penetration of finishes.

Hardware

All hardware used on garden projects—hooks and eyes, screw hooks, braces, hinges, and the like—should be noncorrosive.

Nails

Use only galvanized, aluminum, or stainless steel nails for outdoor projects; other types will rust and stain the wood.

The general rule for choosing nail length is that the nail should be three times as long as the thickness of the part being fastened. Nails that are longer than the total thickness of the parts can be clinched on the back if appearance is not important. Just bend and hammer flush the part of the nail that projects. In fact, clinching nails adds considerable strength to an assembly.

Screws for Softwood

Screw size	Lengths available	Drill required for shank hole frac.	Drill required for pilot hole frac.
# 4	¼"–1½"	⁷⁄₆₄	³⁄₆₄
5	³⁄₈"–1½"	⅛	¹⁄₁₆
6	³⁄₈"–2½"	⁹⁄₆₄	¹⁄₁₆
7	³⁄₈"–2½"	⁵⁄₃₂	¹⁄₁₆
8	³⁄₈"–3"	¹¹⁄₆₄	⁵⁄₆₄
9	½"–3"	³⁄₁₆	⁵⁄₆₄
10	½"–3½"	³⁄₁₆	³⁄₃₂
12	⅝"–4"	⁷⁄₃₂	⁷⁄₆₄
14	¾"–5"	¼	⁷⁄₆₄

Screws and Bolts

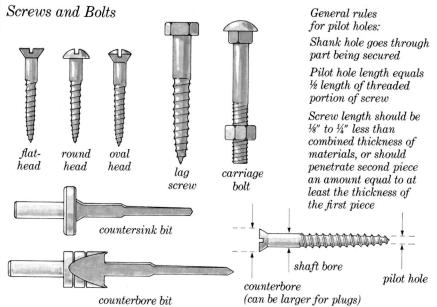

flat-head round head oval head lag screw carriage bolt

countersink bit

counterbore bit

General rules for pilot holes:

Shank hole goes through part being secured

Pilot hole length equals ½ length of threaded portion of screw

Screw length should be ⅛" to ¼" less than combined thickness of materials, or should penetrate second piece an amount equal to at least the thickness of the first piece

shaft bore pilot hole

counterbore (can be larger for plugs)

The chart on page 8 lists the most commonly used nails. Box nails are good to use when the heavier common nails cause wood to split. Common and box nails, because of their broad heads, have more holding power than finishing nails. Use the latter only when you plan to set the nail below the surface of the wood and conceal it with some kind of filler. Stop driving finishing nails before the head is flush, then finish the job with a nail set, sinking the head a maximum of ⅛ inch.

Threaded and ring-shank nails come in all types and sizes and are designed to provide more holding power than nails with plain shanks.

Drive nails with steady strokes, and remember that many light blows will work better than a few strong ones.

Be especially careful not to damage the wood with the last few strokes.

When working with especially brittle or thin wood, or with large nails, make pilot holes before you drive the nails in order to avoid splitting the wood. Blunting tips of nails with a hammer will also help to keep wood from splitting. Avoid driving nails on a common centerline in line with the grain; a staggered nailing pattern is less likely to split wood. Redwood in particular splits easily, but any wood can split, especially if nails are driven close to the edge.

Screws

Screws hold better than nails but require more time to install. Start by drilling the suggested shank and pilot holes listed in the chart above. If you don't have a drill of the right size, choose the one that comes closest on the smaller side. For small screws, you can punch a hole in the wood with an awl, instead of drilling a hole.

Flat-head and oval-head screws require a beveled indent called a countersink. These can be made with a countersink drill after you drill the pilot hole, or you can make both the pilot hole and countersink in one operation with a special tool called a combination countersink bit. It is not necessary to make countersinks in redwood, since the wood is soft enough that screws sink themselves as they are driven.

It is customary with softwoods to stop the countersinking just short of the actual size of the screw head. Driving the screw will sink it far enough to make up the difference. This procedure ensures that the screw will be flush with, not below, the surface of the wood.

Lag screws are very large screws (up to 6 inches long) with square heads or hex-heads that are turned with a wrench. Although they are often used as wood-to-wood connectors, they are especially valuable when a project must be attached to a house, wall, fence, or masonry. In masonry they are used in combination with expansion shields. Lag screws in wood require pilot holes about half the diameter of the screw.

Counterbores. Screws can be concealed with wooden plugs or short lengths of standard dowel. You'll need to drill a counterbore for the plug after you drill the pilot hole. Using the pilot hole as a center, work with a spade bit or a twist drill to enlarge the hole enough to accommodate the dowel. After you have driven the screw, coat the counterbored area with glue and tap in a piece of dowel. Cut off and sand dowel flush after glue dries. Combination counterbore bits, similar to the combination countersink bits described above, enable you to drill both holes in one operation. They come in various sizes so you can

choose one to suit the screws you are working with. Some combination bits come with a companion bit for cutting plugs from the same wood you are using for the project.

Bolts

Bolts are heavy-duty connectors that pull and hold parts together more strongly than either screws or nails. They can be unfastened easily and are good hardware to use for projects you may wish to disassemble. For garden projects, use bolts made of, or coated with, a noncorrosive material.

The most useful bolt for the projects in this book is the carriage bolt. The convex head on the carriage bolt is more decorative than a square head or hex-head. The shoulder under the head, which sinks into and grips the wood, makes it possible for the bolt to be tightened or re-

moved with a single wrench. The length of the bolt should equal the total thickness of the parts being joined, plus about ½ inch for washer and nut. Drill holes that match the diameter of the bolt.

Hinges

Hinges come in a wide variety of types and sizes. Butt hinges come in tight-pin as well as in loose-pin and loose-joint versions for the removal of doors and panels. Don't use the loose kind if security is a factor.

The strap hinge and T hinge are often substituted for the butt hinge on outdoor projects because they add a decorative rustic detail.

Casters

Casters under a container perform two functions: They serve as legs to raise a container off the ground, and they make a container mobile.

Stem varieties lock into sleeves that are positioned in drilled holes. They cost less than plate types but should be used mostly for light-duty applications. Plate casters are attached with screws and can be either fixed or swivel; two of each on a project make it easy to steer. Wheel diameters vary; generally, the larger the wheel, the more weight it will support.

Tools

The tools in the following lists are the ones you'll use most often when building the projects in this book. Since each project requires different tools, read through the directions completely before you begin construction to make sure that you have all the tools needed for that particular project.

Hand Tools

☐ Flexible tape (8' minimum) for measuring and marking
☐ Combination square for measuring, marking cut lines, and checking 90- and 45-degree angles
☐ Framing square for checking right angles during assembly

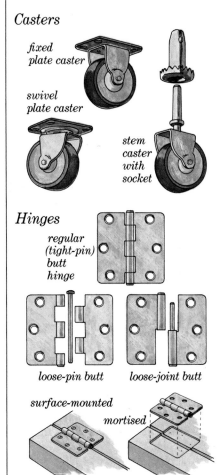

Casters

fixed plate caster

swivel plate caster

stem caster with socket

Hinges

regular (tight-pin) butt hinge

loose-pin butt   *loose-joint butt*

surface-mounted

mortised

☐ Crosscut saw for cutting across the grain of the wood, cutting miters, and cutting plywood

☐ Ripsaw for cutting with wood grain

☐ Deep-frame coping saw for cutting circles and patterns with tight curves

☐ Claw hammer (16 oz) for driving and removing nails up to 8-penny (8d, or 2½ inches)

☐ Framing hammer (20 oz) for driving large nails into 2-by or larger lumber

☐ Nail sets (¹/₁₆", ⅛") for driving nails below surface of wood

☐ Scratch awl for marking dimension points and locations of screw holes and for making pilot holes

☐ Hand drill for making small holes for screws, bolts, and dowels

☐ Push drill with drill points (from ¹/₁₆" to ³/₁₆") for drilling small holes and pilot holes for screws and nails

☐ Set of screwdrivers of varying sizes for driving and removing screws

☐ Wood butt chisels (¼", ½", 1") for joint work and some shaping

☐ Set of open-end wrenches or adjustable wrench, for tightening nuts when using bolts

☐ Socket wrenches for inserting countersunk lag screws

☐ Block plane for rounding corners, beveling, and removing small amounts of wood

☐ Half-round rasp, with handle, for rounding edges and shaping

☐ Sledgehammer for driving stakes

☐ Clamps (bar or pipe clamps and C-clamps) for holding together pieces during assembly

Power Tools

☐ Circular saw makes the same cuts as do crosscut saw and ripsaw; makes angle cuts easier

☐ Saber saw or jigsaw is used primarily for cutting curves

☐ Table saw can make very accurate cuts; can cut large pieces of plywood

☐ Radial-arm saw makes all standard saw cuts, as well as angle cuts, dadoes, and rabbets; with attachments, it can be used as a sander

☐ Electric drill has many uses in addition to drilling (see following)

The first power tool you are likely to buy is a drill. In choosing between a brace and a portable electric drill, consider that the latter is more versatile and is better suited to the finished work required on these projects. You can use it with spade bits, dowel bits, twist drills, and hole saws to form any size hole up to about 2½ inches in diameter. With accessories it's also useful for sanding, wire brushing, rasping, and even mixing paint.

Many of the furniture projects are held together with dowels. A relatively inexpensive tool called a doweling jig facilitates construction of any doweled piece.

Always buy quality tools and keep them clean and sharp. You will gain in the long run because a properly maintained, well-made tool will last indefinitely and will be easier and safer to use.

Working With Tools

Remember to take your time and be alert when working on any project. Read all instructions that come with a tool and follow them—not just at first, but always.

Sawing. Many woodworking problems are caused by poor saw cuts. Take your time, support the work firmly, and take a comfortable stance that permits free and easy strokes. As you near the end of the cut, hold the cut-off piece to avoid splintering.

On long cuts, the kerf (the groove formed by the blade) tends to close and bind the saw. To avoid this, use a chip of wood or a large nail to hold kerf open.

Cuts will be more accurate if you use strips of wood as saw guides. Any straight piece of 1- or 2-inch stock can be clamped or tacked to the work so an edge is on the cut line. The guide lets you cut straight and helps you keep the saw vertical. When possible, stack pieces and clamp them to make duplicate cuts.

A miter box is a very useful sawing accessory. Miter boxes are usually used with backsaws and are available at hardware stores and lumberyards.

Cutting a dado. Many of the projects in this book require dado cuts, which are grooves cut across the grain of a board. It is easiest to cut dadoes with a table or radial-arm saw equipped with a dado blade, but they can also be made with a handsaw or circular saw. Mark both edges of groove, then cut along marks to desired depth. Make several more cuts in between, then remove waste wood with a sharp chisel.

Similar to a dado, a rabbet cut is a groove cut at the end of a board.

Drilling. It's best to clamp your work down, especially when using a power drill. With a nail set or awl, make a small starting hole in the wood; the hole will prevent the bit from skipping across the wood when you begin to drill. Hold the drill steady and perpendicular, and keep the hand that holds the work well out of the path of the bit. Use only enough feed pressure to keep the tool cutting.

Drill speed should decrease as the size of the hole increases. Spade bits are an exception, however—they work best at high speeds regardless of bit size.

Back up the work with scrap wood to prevent splintering. When possible, stack duplicate pieces and drill holes through all at once.

Tool Safety

It makes sense to buy portable electric tools that are double insulated. Extension cords should be heavy-duty and have a grounded connection; repair any frayed cords immediately. Wear safety goggles whenever there's a chance of flying particles, and don't wear loose clothing or work barefoot. Be sure you have adequate ventilation when using any finishing material.

Always use equipment and tools in the proper manner, select the right tool for the job, and make sure tools are well maintained. Following basic safety rules makes woodworking an enjoyable and satisfying experience.

PLANTER BOXES
Simple Box

Here and on the following pages, you will find a collection of wood planting containers to suit a variety of purposes.

The straight, clean lines of this simple planter box make it a natural showcase for a lush display of annuals or perennials.

1. Cut sides (A) and ends (B) from 1 by 6 surfaced redwood or treated lumber. Cut feet (D) from 2 by 4 wood of the same type. Cut base (C) from ¾-inch exterior-grade plywood.

2. Drill five ¾-inch drainage holes in base. Tack rustproof screening over holes to contain dirt.

3. Place feet flush with corners of base and drill pilot holes through base into feet. Attach feet to base with 6-penny (6d) galvanized box nails.

4. Nail ends and then sides to base with 6d nails. (Attach sides and ends so that base is positioned within box as shown in the illustration.) Place nails at least 1 inch from ends of boards to prevent splits.

5. Attach sides to ends with 6d nails. If you use redwood, drill a pilot hole for each nail.

Materials List

1x6 surfaced redwood
2 pieces 16″ long for (A) sides
2 pieces 10½″ long for (B) ends

2x4 surfaced redwood
4 pieces 3½″ long for (D) feet

¾″ exterior-grade plywood
1 piece 10½″x14½″ for (C) base

Hardware and miscellaneous
6d galvanized box nails
Tacks as needed
Rustproof screening (aluminum or fiberglass)

Although simple in design, this planter can add a colorful finishing touch to a deck, windowsill, porch, or walk.

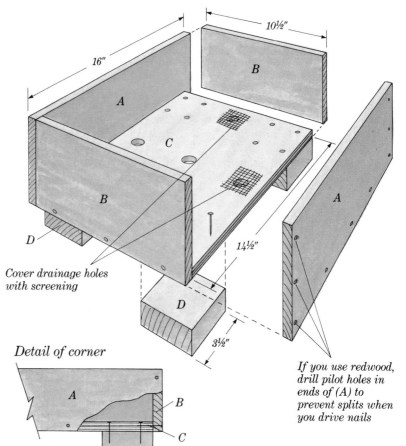

16″

10½″

A

B

C

B

D

14½″

A

3½″

D

Cover drainage holes with screening

Detail of corner

A

B

C

If you use redwood, drill pilot holes in ends of (A) to prevent splits when you drive nails

This easy-to-construct box provides an alternative to clay and plastic containers, and also adds an elegant accent to the garden.

M itered corners give this container a more tailored look than the box-end planters, but are very simple to make. Two different base designs are shown.

1. Cut sides (A) to length, then use a miter box to cut a 45-degree angle at each end of sides. Cut feet (C).

2. Nail all 4 sides together with 8-penny (8d) galvanized box nails. Use 5 nails at each corner—3 driven from 1 side, and 2 from the other (see illustration).

3. Measure and cut base (B) so that it fits within frame. Drill ½-inch or ¾-inch drainage holes and tack screening over them.

4. Align feet with corners of base and attach them with 6d galvanized box nails. Drive nails down through base into feet.

5. Nail base in place through sides with 8d nails.

Alternate Base

Another way to make base is to cut it 1 inch smaller than outside dimension of box and nail it to bottom of frame so it is recessed ½ inch all around (see detail illustration of alternate corner). If you make the base this way, nail on feet after you attach base to sides.

Materials List

2x6 surfaced redwood
4 pieces 18" long for (A) sides

2x4 surfaced redwood
4 pieces 3½" long for (C) feet

¾" exterior-grade plywood
1 piece 15"x15" for (B) base
(or 17"x17" for alternate design)

Hardware and miscellaneous
6d galvanized box nails
8d galvanized box nails
Tacks as needed
Rustproof screening (aluminum or
  fiberglass)

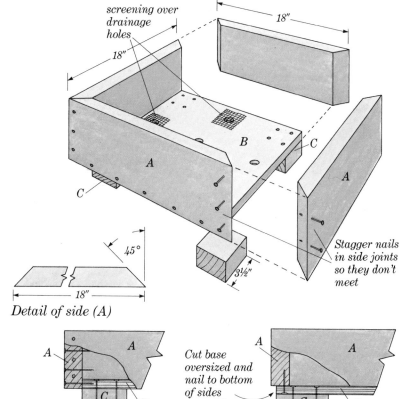

screening over drainage holes

18"

18"

B

C

A

C

A

45°

18"

Detail of side (A)

Stagger nails in side joints so they don't meet

3½"

A

A

C

B

Detail of corner

A

Cut base oversized and nail to bottom of sides set in ½"

A

C

B

Detail of alternate corner

Multipurpose Box

This versatile box can be used with pots of various sizes. The components of the box—dimensioned to suit the container and pot sizes shown on opposite page—include an invertible base and two sleeves of different depths that slip over the projecting corner posts.

Sleeves of either depth may be used, with either base position, depending on the size of pot set in the box. For example, for a 5-gallon can, place the base bottom-down and use the 8-inch sleeve; for low pots, place the base bottom-up and use the 2-inch sleeve.

1. Cut sides (A), ends (B), and legs (D). Nail sides to ends with 8-penny (8d) galvanized box nails. Measure and cut base (C) so that it fits within the square formed by sides and ends.

2. To make leg notches, place base in frame. Then put a leg in each corner with wider face of leg placed against ends. With a pencil, mark outline of leg on base. Cut away wood within outline with a saber saw or handsaw. Drill ½-inch drainage holes in base and tack screening over them.

3. Center legs so that they extend 2 inches above and 2 inches below end pieces. Nail them in place through sides and ends with 8d nails. Insert base into frame and nail it in place through sides and ends.

4. Usually you will use either 1 wide or 1 narrow sleeve per box. You can also make a 6-inch-wide sleeve or not use a sleeve at all, depending on what you plan to put in the box.

For the narrow sleeve, cut sides (E) and ends (F). For the wide sleeve, cut sides (G) and ends (H).

5. Sleeve assembly is easy. Just nail sides to ends with 8d nails.

Materials List

For 1 basic box, 1 narrow sleeve, and 1 wide sleeve

1x6 rough redwood
2 pieces 21" long for (A) sides
2 pieces 19" long for (B) ends

2x4 rough redwood
4 pieces 10" long for (D) legs

¾" exterior-grade plywood
1 piece 19"x19" for (C) base

1x2 rough redwood
2 pieces 21" long for (E) narrow sleeve sides
2 pieces 19" long for (F) narrow sleeve ends

1x8 rough redwood
2 pieces 21" long for (G) wide sleeve sides
2 pieces 19" long for (H) wide sleeve ends

Hardware and miscellaneous
8d galvanized box nails
Tacks as needed
Rustproof screening (aluminum or fiberglass)

Top. *Using the wide sleeve (shown in the center), the box is deep enough to house a plant in a 5-gallon pot.*
Above. *With components for two complete boxes, you can accommodate plants of almost any size. The box in back has been inverted to make a stand for a small marigold.*

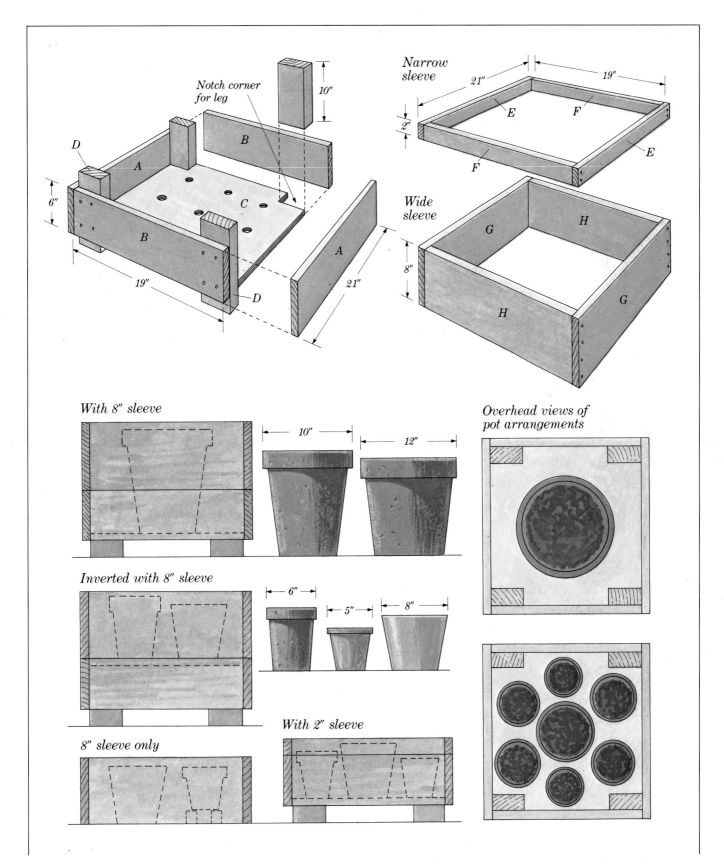

Notch corner
for leg

10"

D

A

B

6"

B

C

A

19"

21"

D

Narrow
sleeve

21"

19"

E

F

2"

F

E

Wide
sleeve

G

H

8"

H

G

With 8" sleeve

10"

12"

Inverted with 8" sleeve

6"

5"

8"

8" sleeve only

With 2" sleeve

Overhead views of
pot arrangements

Carpenter's Toolbox Planter

This attractive redwood planter is light enough to be moved from one place to another. Fill it with annuals or make it into a greenhouse for seedlings.

1. Cut sides (A), ends (B), and handle supports (D) to size.

2. Attach sides to ends with 6-penny (6d) galvanized box nails. Then cut base (C) to fit in frame formed by sides and ends. Drill 6, evenly spaced, ½-inch drainage holes in base and cover them by tacking on rustproof screening.

3. Cut feet (F) to length, place them flush with corners of base, and nail them in place with 6d nails driven through base.

4. Nail base in place with 6d nails through sides and ends.

5. Clamp handle supports together and shape tops with a coping saw to eliminate sharp corners. With pieces still clamped together, drill a 1-inch hole for handle, centered 1¾ inches from top. Then nail a handle support to each end with six 4d galvanized box nails.

6. Cut dowel handle (E) to length and fit it into holes in supports. Drill a pilot hole through each handle support into handle, then secure dowel with 6d nails.

Materials List

1x6 surfaced redwood
2 pieces 20″ long for (A) sides
2 pieces 14″ long for (B) ends

1x4 surfaced redwood
2 pieces 17½″ long for (D) handle supports

¾″ exterior-grade plywood
1 piece 12½x20 for (C) base

2x2 surfaced redwood
4 pieces 3″ long for (F) feet

Hardwood dowel 1″ dia
1 piece 23″ long for (E) handle

Hardware and miscellaneous
4d galvanized box nails
6d galvanized box nails
Tacks as needed
Rustproof screening (aluminum or fiberglass)

Greenhouse Top

You can convert this planter into a miniature greenhouse by cutting ridge support (G), side supports (H), and cover ends (I).

Assemble and attach frame using glue and ¾-inch brads. Using a staple gun, staple heavy plastic (J) to cover ends and drape over frame to form a tent. Fold 1 side back over handle to provide ventilation.

Materials List

**½″x½″ redwood
(or ½″x¾″ trim stock)**
1 piece 21½″ long for (G) ridge support
4 pieces 10″ long for (H) side supports
2 pieces 21″ long for (I) cover ends

Hardware and miscellaneous
¾″ brads
Staples
Waterproof glue
6-mil clear plastic, 21″x21″ for (J)

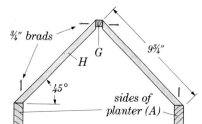

¾″ brads

G

H

9¾″

45°

sides of planter (A)

Optional greenhouse cover

An optional greenhouse frame (shown without plastic cover in the top photograph) extends the uses of this portable planter box.

screening over drainage holes

D

B

A

C

A

F

F

F

F

B

20″

14″

I

G

H

I

J

H

H

E

17½″

D

Reminiscent of an old pickle barrel, this rustic planter is easier to make than it looks. It is raised off the ground by four legs made of long staves. To make this project, you'll need a table saw or radial-arm saw with a dado attachment.

1. From ½-inch exterior-grade plywood, cut the 18-inch-diameter base (C). Drill several ½-inch drainage holes and cover them by tacking on rustproof screening.

2. To cut staves, set saw blade for a 9-degree bevel-cut and fence for a 3-inch width. This project goes faster if you cut bevels on stave boards before cutting boards to length. Then cut short staves (A) to 8 inches and long staves (B) to 11 inches.

3. Set up dado head to make two ½-inch-wide by ¼-inch-deep cuts in each stave to hold banding. Make these cuts on outside (wider) faces of all staves. Cuts should be 1½ inches from top and 6 inches from top.

4. Reset dado head to make a ⁹⁄₁₆-inch-wide by ⅜-inch-deep dado to hold plywood base. Make this cut on inside (narrower) faces of all staves, 6¾ inches from top.

5. Temporarily staple together 4 sections, each containing 1 long stave and 4 short staves. Band sections together around base with string or masking tape. Barrel can be held together permanently using any of the following 3 methods.

☐ Tack flat metal or plastic banding to one stave, pull tight around others using pliers, and tack in place (see photograph).

☐ Wrap wire or metal clothesline around the barrel 2 or 3 times; staple or tack ends in place.

☐ Cut plastic or cotton clothesline into two 12-foot pieces. Fold one piece in half and twist line together to form a loop at folded end. Wrap line around lower groove. Pass ends

through loop, bend them back, and pull as tight as possible with a pair of pliers. Hold ends in place with a couple of galvanized staples. Band upper groove in the same way.

6. If desired, paint strapping with flat-black enamel paint.

Materials List

½" exterior-grade plywood
1 piece 18" dia for (C) base

1x3 rough redwood
16 pieces 8" long for (A) short staves
4 pieces 11" long for (B) long staves

Hardware and miscellaneous
Galvanized staples
Tacks
Rustproof screening (aluminum or fiberglass)
String or masking tape
Banding material:
    12' flat plastic or metal strapping, or 32' galvanized wire or metal clothesline, or 24' plastic or cotton clothesline
Flat-black enamel paint (optional)

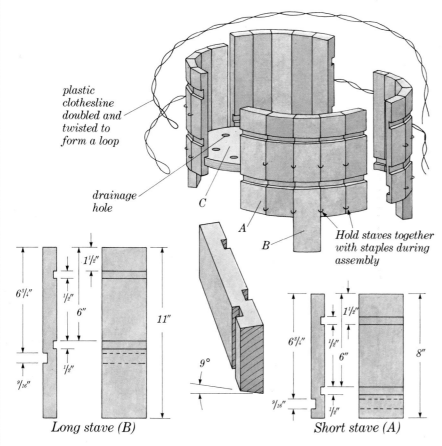

plastic clothesline doubled and twisted to form a loop

drainage hole

C

A

B

Hold staves together with staples during assembly

1½"

6¾"

½"

6"

½"

⁹⁄₁₆"

11"

Long stave (B)

9°

1½"

6¾"

½"

6"

½"

⁹⁄₁₆"

8"

Short stave (A)

This Barrel Planter is actually less than a foot tall, but the design can be altered to fit many types of plants.

Grandpa Fabri's Planter

This portable planter, designed with long-bolt connectors for strength, is easy to assemble. It is quite large, but can be rolled from place to place on casters.

1. Cut sides (A) and ends (B) to length. On sides, make a mark 4¼ inches in from each bottom corner. Draw a line connecting this point to top corner, and cut sides at an angle along line.

2. Drill five ½-inch bolt holes in each side as shown in the illustration. Clamp sides together and drill holes through both at once to save time. Fasten sides and ends together with 8-penny (8d) galvanized box nails.

3. Measure and cut base (C) to fit within sides and ends. Drill ½- or ¾-inch drainage holes. Nail base to sides and ends with 8d nails.

4. Cut five 18-inch-long pieces of threaded rod (D) with a hacksaw. You'll need a small metal file to smooth cut ends of rods. Insert rods and secure with washers and nuts. Screw fixed casters on one end of planter and swivel casters on other end. Tack screening over drainage holes and add soil and plants.

Materials List

1x12 surfaced redwood
2 pieces 58" long for (A) sides
2 pieces 14" long for (B) ends

¾" exterior-grade plywood
1 piece 14"x46" long for (C) base

½" threaded rod stock
5 pieces 18" long for (D) tie rods

Hardware and miscellaneous
8d galvanized box nails
10 hex nuts ½", washers
4 plate casters with ⅝" screws (2 fixed-wheel and 2 swivel for better steering)
Tacks as needed
Rustproof screening (aluminum or fiberglass)

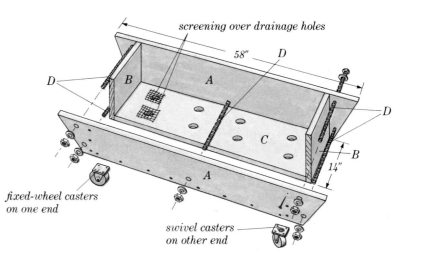

At 5 feet long by 1 foot deep, this container is large enough to house a healthy crop of vegetables.

screening over drainage holes
58"
fixed-wheel casters on one end
swivel casters on other end

Detail of side (A)

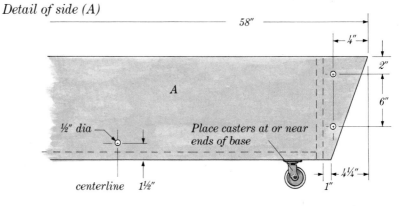

58"
4"
2"
6"
A
½" dia
Place casters at or near ends of base
centerline   1½"
4¼"
1"

This handsome redwood planter is raised off the ground by steel post anchors, which can be purchased at most lumberyards and building-supply stores.

1. Cut the sides (A) and ends (B). Drill ⅞-inch holes and cut 1-inch bevels on corners (see illustration). Mark position of ends on side pieces and fasten ends in position with 8-penny (8d) galvanized box nails.

2. Rip-cut filler blocks (D) to 2¾-inch width from 4 by 4 stock, then cut them to length. You can also make filler blocks by rip-cutting 4 pieces of ¾-inch stock to the 2¾-inch width and nailing them together to form each block. Be sure nails are near edges so they won't interfere with bolts inserted later. For filler blocks, only the 9-inch length and the 2¾-inch dimension between side and post anchor are critical. The other width of block can vary from 2¾ inches to 3½ inches or so.

3. Measure and cut base (C) to fit. Notch corners to fit around filler blocks and post anchors (G) and drill ½-inch or ¾-inch drainage holes. Nail base in place with 8d nails.

4. Using 8d nails, attach filler blocks to corners so that bottoms are flush with underside of base and tops are about 2¼ inches below rim of planter. If filler blocks are pieced together, check that nails won't interfere with bolts.

5. Slide post-anchor legs (G) into place and mark position of bolt holes on sides. Drill ⅜-inch holes through sides and filler blocks, then bolt legs in place.

6. Insert pipe handles (E) and secure with pipe caps (F).

7. Before filling with soil, tack rustproof screening over drainage holes.

8. If desired, paint metal parts of planter. Use black paint to give it the look of wrought iron, or apply a bright color.

Materials List

1x12 surfaced redwood
2 pieces 28" long for (A) sides
2 pieces 14" long for (B) ends

4x4 surfaced redwood
4 pieces 9" long for (D) filler blocks
or 16 pieces 9" long if using 1x4 surfaced redwood

¾" exterior-grade plywood
1 piece 14"x20½" for (C) base

4 steel post anchors 4"x4"
There are several styles of post anchors; find ones that look like (G) legs in the illustration.

½" dia galvanized water pipe
2 pieces 17" long, threaded at both ends, for (E) handles (have these cut and threaded at a hardware store or plumbers' supply), with 4 galvanized pipe caps (F) ½" dia

Hardware and miscellaneous
8d galvanized box nails
8 hex-head bolts ⅜"x4½", nuts, washers
Tacks as needed
Rustproof screening (aluminum or fiberglass)
Rust-inhibiting paint (optional)

The metal legs on this planter give it a distinctive look and lend themselves to decorative coats of paint.

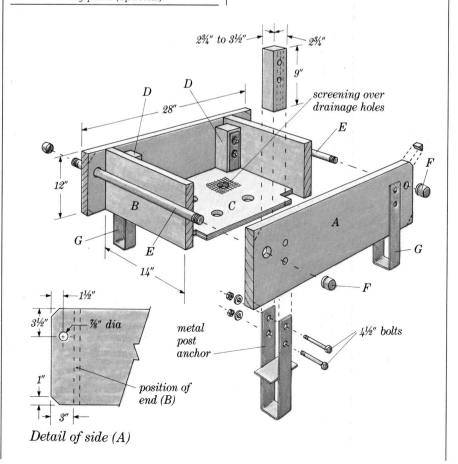

Detail of side (A)

Pagoda Planter

Construction of this oriental-style planter will be easier if you use a table saw or radial-arm saw with a dado attachment.

1. Cut sides (A) to 5 inches by 13 inches and slats (B) to 5 inches.

2. Set up saw to make a ⅜-inch-wide by ⅝-inch-deep dado cut. Clamp all 4 sides together and, along each edge, cut ⅝-inch-deep slots 1 inch down from top, 4½ inches down from top, 1 inch up from bottom, and 4½ inches up from bottom.

3. From 1 by 10 surfaced redwood, cut a piece 8¼ inches square for base (C). Cut off corners so sides are about 5 inches long. Drill ½-inch or ¾-inch drainage holes.

4. Glue and nail sides to base with 4-penny (4d) galvanized box nails, then glue slats into slots. Use a square to be sure sides stay plumb as you work.

5. If you plan to hang the planter, drill a ¼-inch hole ¾ inch from top of each side and string sturdy ropes through holes.

6. Line planter with black plastic, fill with soil mix, and plant through slits cut in plastic. Poke drainage holes in plastic through holes in base.

Materials List

½ x6 or ¾ x6 surfaced redwood
4 pieces 13" long for (A) sides

⅜ x1 surfaced redwood
16 pieces 5" long for (B) slats

1x10 surfaced redwood
1 piece 8¼" square for (C) base

Hardware and miscellaneous
4d galvanized box nails
Waterproof glue
4-mil black plastic as needed
¼" dia rope as needed

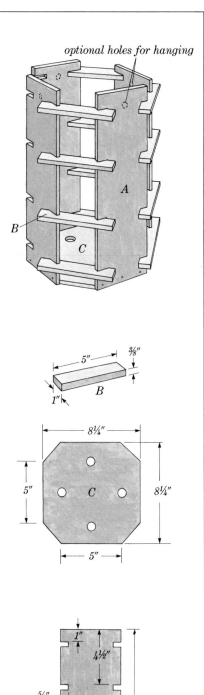

optional holes for hanging

Blossoms cascade from the vertical openings in this simple octagonal container. It is particularly attractive as a hanging planter.

Redwood blocks are easy to put together, and their pattern and texture make a contrasting backdrop for plants.

Here is an attractive planter made of 1 by 2 redwood. The directions are for a planter of either 9 or 13 layers, but you can make it as deep as you like.

1. Using a coping saw or power saber saw, cut a 16-inch-diameter circle for the base (B). Drill several ½-inch drainage holes and tack rustproof screening over them.

2. If you have a table saw, set a stop block at 5 inches for quick cutting of the 72 or 104 redwood blocks (A). If not, use a miter box with a piece of wood clamped in it to form a stop.

3. Glue and nail blocks to base. Outside corners of blocks should touch perimeter of base; inside corners should touch adjacent blocks. Attach with waterproof glue and 3-penny (3d) galvanized box nails. Nail and glue second layer so ends meet in middle of blocks in first layer. Continue until all blocks are used.

4. Line planter with plastic. Attach casters, or hang by threading ends of a 3-wire pot hanger around blocks in second or third layer from top (see illustration).

Materials List

¾″ exterior-grade plywood
1 piece 16″ dia for (B) base

1x2 surfaced redwood
72 pieces 5″ long for (A) sides (for 9 layers) or 104 pieces 5″ long (for 13 layers)

Hardware and miscellaneous
3d galvanized box nails
Waterproof glue
3-wire pot hanger or 3 plate casters (2 fixed wheel, 1 swivel)
4-mil black plastic as needed
Tacks as needed
Rustproof screening (aluminum or fiberglass)

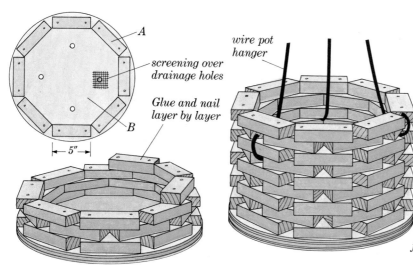

fixed-wheel caster   swivel caster

Wheelbarrow Planter

This decorative yard ornament is a functional planter, too. You'll need a hole saw on your drill to make this project.

1. Cut sides (A) and ends (B) and nail them together with 6-penny (6d) galvanized box nails. Cut base (C) to fit within box. Drill several ½-inch or ¾-inch drainage holes, and cover them by tacking on screening. Nail base in place with 6d nails.

2. Cut handles (D), front brace (E), and legs (F) to size. Drill ¼-inch holes where shown on illustrations of each piece *except* holes marked X (drill these later). Cut bevels in legs. Shape about 6 to 8 inches of handle ends with a knife or rasp to form comfortable and attractive grips.

3. Turn box upside down and place front brace (E) flush with front edge of base and centered. Drill holes through base to match holes in brace. Lay handles on brace so that holes 13 inches from ends of handles line up with holes through brace and box. Bolt box, brace, and handles with ¼-inch by 4¼-inch stove bolts.

4. Position legs (F) against back of box so beveled ends are flush with top and outside edges are 1½ inches from outside edges of box. Drill holes through back of box to match those in legs. Bolt each leg to box with two ¼-inch by 2¾-inch stove bolts.

5. Pivot each handle so it rests against outside of each leg and touches base of box. Drill ¼-inch holes (X) horizontally through handles and legs as shown. Bolt them together with ¼-inch by 3½-inch stove bolts.

6. Cut wheel pieces (G) and wheel braces (H). Place wheel pieces side by side and attach 2 braces to each side of wheel with seven 1¾-inch by No. 8 flat-head wood screws per brace. Make sure braces are at least 2½ inches apart as shown. Mark center of wheel on wheel pieces and scribe a circle with a 5¼-inch radius. Use a 2-inch hole saw to make axle hole in center of wheel, then cut outside edge of wheel with a coping saw or power saber saw.

This rustic Wheelbarrow Planter can be rolled from one place to another to show off plants or to let them catch some elusive sun.

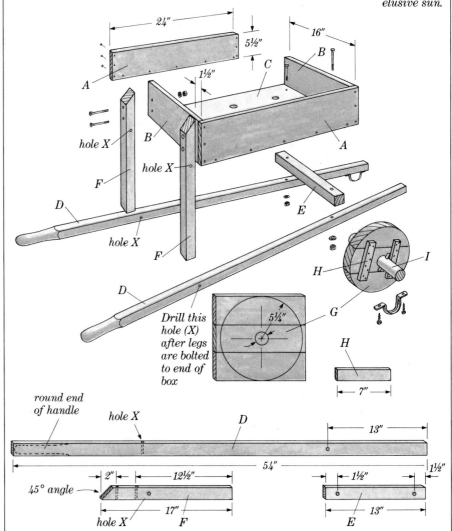

7. Cut axle (I), and sand it and hole in wheel so wheel turns on axle. Drill two ¼-inch holes through axle, each centered 1¼ inches from the midpoint. Cut axle pins (J), glue one pin so it is centered in one of the small holes, slip on wheel, and glue second pin in other hole. Pins help keep wheel centered on axle when wheelbarrow is rolled.

8. Fasten axle tightly to handles with 2-inch pipe clamps, and the wheelbarrow is ready to roll.

Materials List

1x6 surfaced redwood
2 pieces 24" long for (A) sides
2 pieces 16" long for (B) ends

¾" exterior-grade plywood
1 piece 16"x22½" for (C) base

2x2 surfaced redwood
2 pieces 54" long for (D) handles
1 piece 13" long for (E) front brace
2 pieces 17" long for (F) legs

2x4 surfaced redwood
3 pieces 12" long for (G) wheel

1x2 surfaced redwood
4 pieces 7" long for (H) wheel braces

2" dia hardwood dowel
1 piece 9" long for (I) axle

¼" dia hardwood dowel
2 pieces 2½" long for (J) axle pins

Hardware and miscellaneous
6d galvanized box nails
32 flat-head wood screws 1¾"x#8
2 stove bolts ¼"x4¼", nuts, washers
4 stove bolts ¼"x2¾", nuts, washers
2 stove bolts ¼"x3½", nuts, washers
2 galvanized pipe clamps 2" with
  1" round-head wood screws
Waterproof glue
Tacks as needed
Rustproof screening (aluminum or
  fiberglass)

Y ou can make another version of the planter on page 21 by cutting a 30-degree angle on the ends of the side pieces. When set on the base, they form a hexagon with precisely mitered joints. Add as many layers as you like, from 7 (as shown in photograph) to 12 or more.

1. Using a coping saw or power saber saw, cut a 16-inch-diameter circle for the base (B). Drill several ½-inch drainage holes.

2. Cut side pieces (A). Using a jig such as the one shown on page 25 will speed up cutting of the 30-degree miters. To make and use jig, see instructions under step 1 on page 25.

3. Attach side pieces to base with glue and 3-penny (3d) galvanized box nails. Stagger each layer of blocks over previous one.

4. Attach plate casters if desired. Line planter with black plastic and fill with soil, or use it to hide a large pot.

The Mitered Hexagon Planter is a neater, more finished version of the Layered Planter on page 21.

Materials List

¾" exterior-grade plywood
1 piece 16" dia for (B) base

1x2 surfaced redwood
42 pieces 9" long for (A) sides (for
  7 layers) or 72 pieces 9" long (for
  12 layers)

Hardware and miscellaneous
3d galvanized box nails
3 plate casters (2 fixed wheel, 1 swivel),
  with screws
Waterproof glue
4-mil black plastic (optional)

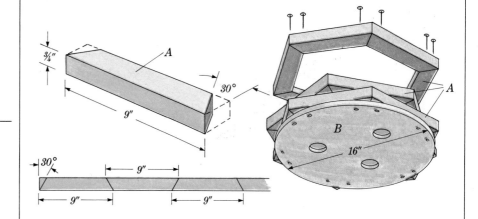

Hide-a-Can Box

Many kinds of plants grow well in their nursery cans for months or years. If you prefer a neater, more finished look but don't want to transplant, the solution is to cover the can with a decorative box.

Supplies needed for boxes of four different sizes are listed. Check diameter and height of your container when deciding which box to make.

1. Cut sides, top pieces, frame, and cleats for the box you want to make.

1-gallon planter (holds a can 8" high by 7" wide)

Lath: 33 pieces 8¾" long (sides and top)
1x2: 8 pieces 8" long (frame)
      2 pieces 7¼" long (cleats)

2-gallon planter (holds a can 9" high by 9¼" wide)

Lath: 36 pieces 9¾" long (sides)
      9 pieces 11" long (top)
1x2: 8 pieces 10¼" long (frame)
      2 pieces 9½" long (cleats)

5-gallon planter (holds a can 13" high by 12¾" wide)

Lath: 48 pieces 13¾" long (sides)
      12 pieces 14½" long (top)
1x2: 8 pieces 13¾" long (frame)
      2 pieces 13" long (cleats)

15-gallon planter (holds a can 18½" high by 15¼" wide)

Lath: 56 pieces 19¼" long (sides)
      14 pieces 17¼" long (top)
1x2: 8 pieces 16½" long (frame)
      2 pieces 15¾" long (cleats)

2. Assemble sides by nailing slats for each side (A) to 2 frame pieces (B) with 2-penny (2d) galvanized box nails. The first slat should be flush with ends of frame pieces; all slat ends should overhang sides of frame pieces by ¼ inch. Use a framing square to keep sides square as you nail. Do not nail last slat onto each side; allow a little of each frame piece to extend beyond next-to-last slat.

3. Nail sides together with 8d galvanized box nails. When all sides are joined, put last slat on each side. Hold slat in place, and if it extends past adjacent side, mark and cut it so it is flush. Then nail in place with 2d nails.

4. Nail top slats (C) to cleats (D) with 2d nails. Let first slat overhang cleat ends by ¾ inch, and let slat ends overhang cleat sides by ¾ inch. Nail

on half of slats, then start over at other end of cleats and repeat process, working toward middle. If last slat doesn't fit (and it probably won't) cut it with a ripsaw or utility knife.

5. Mark hole in center of top with a compass or by tracing around a can, then cut top in two by cutting cleats between slats near midline. Next, cut out hole with a coping saw or power saber saw. If cutting hole entails cutting all the way through some top slats, you may want to attach cut pieces to adjacent whole slats with short scrap pieces.

Materials List
For all boxes

¼ x1½ redwood lath
for (A) sides and (C) top

1x2 surfaced redwood
for (B) frame and (D) cleats

Hardware and miscellaneous
2d galvanized box nails
8d galvanized box nails

Hide-a-Can Boxes are easy to construct and are made of inexpensive lath or scrap sticks available at most lumberyards.

Top

Cut top cleats between slats

Cut hole for stem

Rip last slat to fit if necessary

waste

C

D

Overhang slats ¾" on ends

D

Overhang ¾" on both ends of slats

2d nails

8d nails

waste

Side

Don't nail on last slat until box assembly

A

B

B

First slat is flush with ends of frame

Overhang ¼" on both ends of slats

framing square

Rip last slat for each side so it overlaps first slat on adjoining side

The photograph shows this project made with ¾-inch-square redwood trim stock, which is available at many building suppliers. It can, however, be made less expensively with 1 by 1 rough redwood or any other square stock of similar size.

1. Begin by making a jig to cut angles on ends of side pieces. Nail scrap 1 by 3 to each side of a 1-foot-long piece of the square stock you are using. Make two 60-degree-angle cuts 9 inches apart through sides down to base. Then cut the 96 side pieces (A) by putting stock into jig and using saw cuts as guides.

Save time and lumber by turning stock over each time you make a cut and lining up newly cut edge with one saw guide. You need only make one new cut for each piece.

2. Assemble by toenailing the first layer of side pieces to a temporary base of scrap plywood with 3-penny (3d) galvanized box nails. Use only 1 nail per piece, and don't nail in completely. Glue and nail on several layers, then remove temporary base and continue adding layers until all pieces are used.

3. For the lid, cut enough top pieces (B) to cover top and hang over edge by about 1 inch (cut them to a rough length). Then assemble lid in 2 halves. Glue and nail top pieces together with 3d nails as you did sides. Estimate where the plant opening will be and where the edges will be cut. Keep nails away from these areas where you will saw later.

4. Center rough lid on hexagon and trace hexagon shape on it. Cut lid ½ inch outside this line. Mark hole in center of lid with a compass or by tracing around a can or jar. Cut with a coping saw or power saber saw.

5. Cut 4 top cleats (C) and nail in place so they keep lid centered on hexagon.

Materials List

¾ x ¾ redwood trim stock (or 1x1 rough redwood or other stock)
96 pieces 9″ long for (A) sides
24 pieces 17″ long for (B) top
4 pieces 6″ long for (C) top cleats

Hardware and miscellaneous
3d galvanized box nails
Waterproof glue

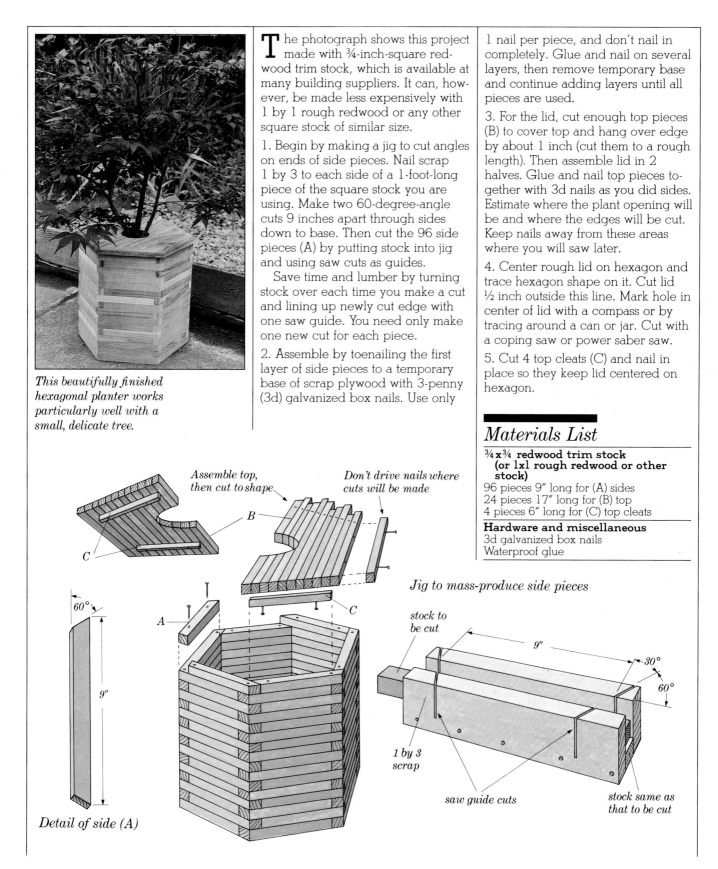

This beautifully finished hexagonal planter works particularly well with a small, delicate tree.

Assemble top, then cut to shape

Don't drive nails where cuts will be made

Jig to mass-produce side pieces

stock to be cut

1 by 3 scrap

saw guide cuts

stock same as that to be cut

60°

9″

Detail of side (A)

RAISED BEDS
Bench Raised Bed

There are many good reasons to build raised beds. They are attractive and provide an easy way to level or terrace a sloping garden. Raised beds can also help you solve the problem of indigenous soil that is too sandy or rocky, or has too much clay or a shallow hardpan that doesn't allow it to drain.

If the soil in your garden will not easily support an annual vegetable or flower garden, a raised bed may be the best solution. Raised beds have another big advantage—especially in areas where winters are cold. In a cool, wet spring, the soil in a raised bed will drain, warm up, and be ready for planting weeks before the regular garden soil can be worked and seeded. This means you can enjoy your corn and tomatoes sooner.

Raised beds are no more than large, bottomless boxes. The sides and ends can be made of 1-inch or 2-inch redwood, cedar, or other decay-resistant wood, railroad ties, old telephone poles, brick, or concrete. The bed illustrated here is made of 2-inch redwood stock.

Beds can be 12 to 16 inches high, secured with lag screws or carriage bolts to 4 by 4 corner posts. The posts can be extended into the soil for anchorage or cut at grade. Projects as large as 4 feet by 10 feet can be made using corner-post construction. If your bed is larger, add intermediate posts for additional strength and extend them into the soil; posts will not provide lateral support if attached only to the sides.

If a raised bed is to be accessible from both sides, a width of 6 feet is practical; planting, weeding, and

harvesting can be done without walking in the bed. If a raised bed will be accessible from only one side, make it 3 to 4 feet wide.

Beds should be 12 to 16 inches above grade to allow enough depth for the root systems of plants. Since soil is expensive, don't make beds deeper than necessary.

After building a box, you may want to add a cap to improve the appearance. Use 2-by surfaced stock and secure it to the sides with 16-penny (16d) galvanized common or box nails. You can either butt or miter the corners. Mitered corners look better and allow you to nail both pieces to the corner posts for extra strength. Wider seats on one or more sides, as shown on the Bench Raised Bed, are a practical addition.

This Bench Raised Bed measures 4 feet by 10 feet, but the dimensions can easily be altered to suit your particular needs. Side seats, running the length of the bed, make weeding less of a chore.

1. Cut sides (A), ends (B), corner posts (C), side posts (D), and end caps (G). Cut seats (F) from 12-foot 2 by 8s. Cut the scrap 2 by 8 pieces into four 5¼-inch squares, then cut squares diagonally to make the 8 triangular seat braces (H).

2. Attach corner posts to ends (B) using ⅜-inch by 4-inch lag screws and washers. Position top screw 4 inches from top of end so it will not interfere with end support (E). Drill ³/₁₆-inch pilot holes. Insert screws and tighten them using a socket or crescent wrench.

Corners for Raised Beds

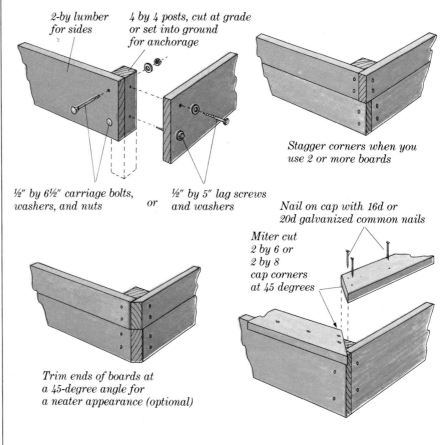

2-by lumber for sides

4 by 4 posts, cut at grade or set into ground for anchorage

½" by 6½" carriage bolts, washers, and nuts

or

½" by 5" lag screws and washers

Stagger corners when you use 2 or more boards

Trim ends of boards at a 45-degree angle for a neater appearance (optional)

Nail on cap with 16d or 20d galvanized common nails

Miter cut 2 by 6 or 2 by 8 cap corners at 45 degrees

3. Nail end seat braces flush with tops and ends of sides by driving 16-penny (16d) galvanized box nails through sides into braces. Position braces so grain runs vertically.

4. Attach sides to corner posts, positioning each side flush with outsides of ends (B). Offset lag screws to clear end-to-post screws.

5. Position frame in garden site. Dig oversized postholes for side posts, a little over 1 foot deep, outside the center of each side. Attach side posts to sides with lag screws as you did corner posts, flush with top of sides. Screw them in place from the inside. Backfill holes with tamped-down earth or concrete.

6. Measure distance across ends between tips of seat braces. Cut end supports (E) to this length, then miter their ends at 45 degrees. Nail end supports to ends with 16d nails. Check that supports are flush with top edge and centered across ends. Secure to each end seat brace with two ¼-inch by 2¾-inch lag screws and washers. Nail the 4 middle seat braces to side posts, flush with top of sides, with 16d nails.

7. Set seats in place and nail them to sides, seat braces, and side posts with 16d nails. Set nails with a large nail set. Position end caps flush with ends of seats, and nail them to ends. Sand edges of seat boards smooth.

This design integrates garden seating with a raised bed that shows off flowers and makes tending plants easier.

Materials List

2x12 rough redwood
2 pieces 120″ long for (A) sides
2 pieces 48″ long for (B) ends

4x4 rough redwood
4 pieces 12″ long for (C) corner posts
2 pieces 24″ long for (D) side posts

2x4 surfaced redwood
2 pieces 48″ long for (G) end caps
2 pieces approximately 62½″ long for (E) end supports

2x8 surfaced redwood
2 pieces 123″ long for (F) seats
4 pieces 5¼″x5¼″ for (H) seat braces

Hardware and miscellaneous
16d galvanized box nails
20 lag screws ⅜″x4″, washers
8 lag screws ¼″x2¾″, washers
Concrete (optional)

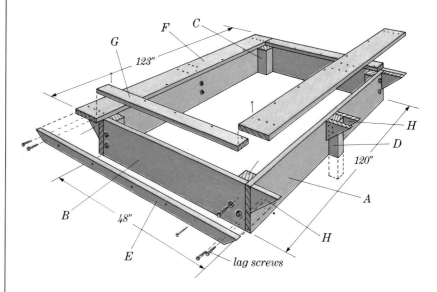

Free-form Raised Bed

This type of raised bed is usually only 5 or 6 inches deep—made of 1 by 8, 1 by 6, or narrower lumber—and is therefore used as a design element rather than a method of improving soil or solving other problems.

Traditionally, lumber is bent with steam, but kerfing is more practical for the homeowner. This technique works on either 1-by or 2-by lumber and is especially effective for gentle, wide-sweeping curves in a garden.

Keep kerf depth to about three quarters of the thickness of the stock, and space cuts 1 or 2 inches apart. For a sharper curve, you can add more kerfs between those already cut, but too many will weaken the lumber. Wetting the wood, especially the unkerfed side, will help to prevent cracking.

If you cut kerfs with a radial-arm saw, mark spacing of kerfs on the fence so you can move the lumber quickly and precisely without measuring after each cut. If you are using a portable circular saw, make a gauge (see illustration) from a piece of scrap wood and two small finishing nails. The gauge keeps kerfs parallel and evenly spaced and saves time.

To use this gauge, measure and cut the first few kerfs freehand. Then set the gauge on the board with the nails inserted in a kerf, and run the base plate of the saw along the guide edge of the gauge to make a cut. Reset the gauge in the next kerf, make a cut, and continue the procedure.

Bend the kerfed board and nail it to 1 by 2 stakes 8 to 12 inches long. Redwood stakes are sold for this purpose; if you use another kind of wood, treat it with a preservative. Keep stakes and kerfs inside the bed where they'll be covered with soil. To hide tops of stakes, drive them flush with the board and cut them off at a 45-degree angle.

The easiest way to nail the board to a stake is to hold the head of a sledgehammer against the back of the stake with your foot and nail through the board into the stake.

Sturdy, curving garden borders can be made from lengths of 1- or 2-inch lumber that has been kerfed.

Kerfing Boards for a Raised Bed

small finishing nails

a little less than depth of kerf

guide edge

kerfs   *gauge*   *saw blade*

To be exactly even, kerf spacing must be an even division of distance between saw blade and guide nails (for example, ⅓, as shown, ¼, ½)

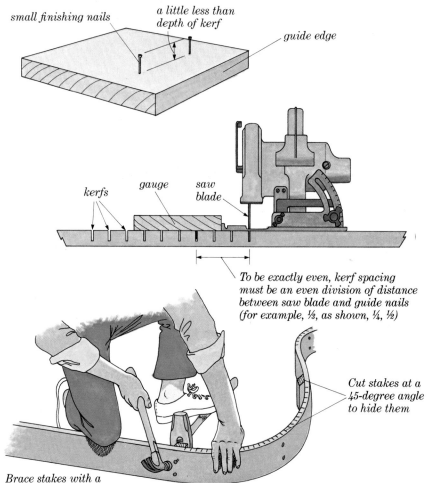

Cut stakes at a 45-degree angle to hide them

Brace stakes with a sledgehammer while nailing through board

Bender Board

You can make a low raised bed without kerfing by using bender board, which can be purchased at home and garden centers. For a long-lasting bed, use bender board made of heartwood of redwood, cedar, or cypress; sapwood will rot sooner in the ground.

Drive wood stakes into the ground to form the shape of the bed, and gradually bend the first board around the stakes. Wetting the wood helps to avoid cracking. Use enough nails to hold the board in place, then put in additional stakes so there is 1 every 3 feet (closer on curves) and at every joint. Then add a second board, staggering joints and adding more stakes as necessary. Add a third layer of boards if desired. Nail all boards to the stakes with 6-penny (6d) or 8-penny (8d) galvanized box nails.

Toenail the bender boards together to keep them from spreading with age. With a sledgehammer behind the boards, drive a nail through all boards at a 45-degree angle. When the nail hits the hammer head, it will turn and clinch itself into the wood.

Railroad Ties

Railroad ties or any square timbers (4 by 4 or 6 by 6) also make attractive raised beds. Instead of using posts at the corners, stagger pieces like logs in a traditional log cabin. Anchor this kind of bed by driving lengths of ½-inch pipe into the ground through ⅞-inch holes made with an auger in the first layer of timbers.

Subsequent layers of wood can be held together with pipe, or they can be toenailed together with 16d or 20d galvanized common nails. The bed will look better if all nailing is done on the back side and between timbers so heads are hidden.

You may want to add a surfaced 2 by 6 (or wider) seat, as in the Bench Raised Bed (page 26), to sit on and to protect yourself and your clothing from the creosote that usually saturates railroad ties.

Raised beds can be made from many kinds of materials, from heavy planks to thin bender board, depending on what is available and the effect desired.

Raised Beds From Railroad Ties

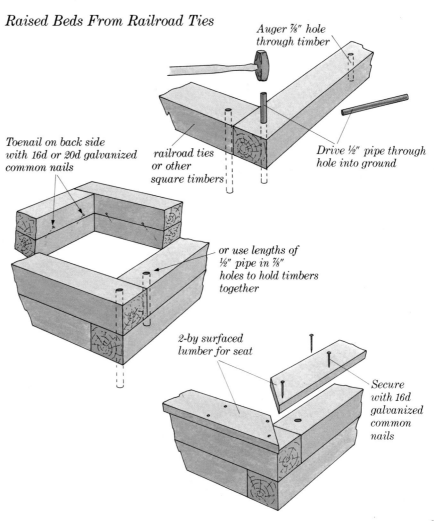

Auger ⅞" hole through timber

Toenail on back side with 16d or 20d galvanized common nails

railroad ties or other square timbers

Drive ½" pipe through hole into ground

or use lengths of ½" pipe in ⅞" holes to hold timbers together

2-by surfaced lumber for seat

Secure with 16d galvanized common nails

Putterer's Garden

The waist-high Putterer's Garden is easy to build and allows you to tend plants comfortably, without stooping. It features a convenient storage shelf and a drip catcher to divert water runoff away from shelf.

As with the other raised beds, construction is simple. You can vary the dimensions of this basic bed to fit your needs, and you can easily build a custom version using the Ideas to Build On, on the following pages. Because the bed is heavy, it should be constructed near where you plan to use it.

1. Cut sides (A), ends (B), stretchers (G), and legs (D). Attach ends to legs with ½-inch by 4½-inch lag screws as shown in the illustration. Position legs so they are flush with outside edges of ends and 2 inches below top edges of ends. Drill ¼-inch pilot holes for screws through ends into legs.

2. Set both end assemblies on their sides and attach side pieces (A) to legs so they are flush with end pieces (B). Again drill ¼-inch pilot holes for lag screws. With unit still on its side, attach stretchers (G) to legs with 16-penny (16d) galvanized box nails.

3. Set whole unit upright and install the 5 base supports (E) and 5 shelf supports (H). Cut base supports so they fit exactly between sides, and shelf supports so they fit between stretchers. Note that base supports are positioned flat, while shelf supports are on edge. Nail them in place with 16d nails, spaced approximately as shown in the illustration. Base supports should be flush with bottom of sides. Drive nails through sides and stretchers into supports.

4. Next, install cleats (F) between base supports. Cut 8 pieces of 1 by 2 stock to fit exactly between base supports and nail them in place with 8d galvanized box nails. Top edges of cleats must be flush with top edges of supports so plywood base will rest evenly on all its support pieces.

5. Cut and install drip frame pieces (J and K), nailing them to legs with 8d nails. Attach drip frame sides (J) to outside of legs. Attach drip frame ends (K) to inside of legs at an angle so their tops are tangent to tops of long pieces. With a staple gun, attach heavy-gauge plastic to the frame, pulling it taut as you go. Staple into bottom of frame pieces for a neater appearance.

6. Cut plywood base (C) and shelf (I) so that they fit exactly within sides and ends. Notch corners to fit around legs and nail shelf and base to their support members with 8d nails.

7. Drill ½-inch drainage holes in base about 8 inches apart and tack screening over them. The bed in the photograph has been coated with a stain; you may want to protect yours with a wood preservative, or line it with heavy plastic with drainage holes cut in it. See page 8 for information on wood finishes.

This large raised bed makes gardening easier on the back. If built at the width indicated, plants are easily accessible from both sides of the bed. Here, two beds have been placed end to end.

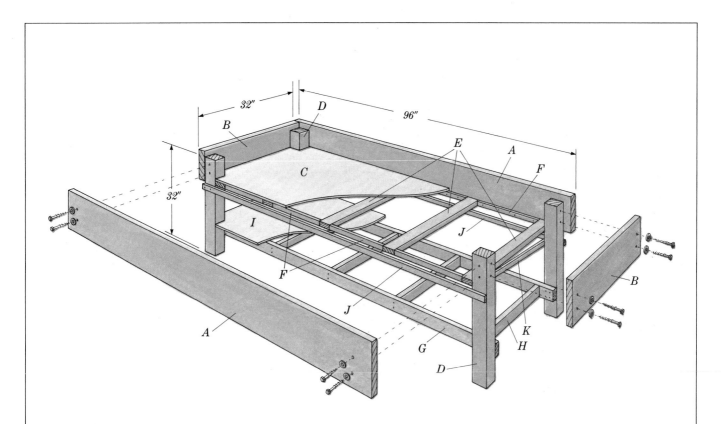

*Sloping plastic sheet under
the bed keeps drainage off
storage shelf below.*

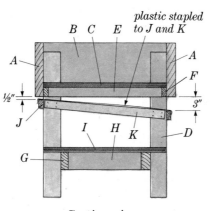

plastic stapled
to J and K

Section view

Materials List

2x12 rough redwood
2 pieces 96" long for (A) sides
2 pieces 32" long for (B) ends

2x4 rough redwood
2 pieces 92" long for (G) stretchers
5 pieces 32" long for (E) base supports
5 pieces 20" long for (H) shelf supports

4x4 rough redwood
4 pieces 32" long for (D) legs

1x2 rough redwood
8 pieces 16" long for (F) cleats
2 pieces 92" long for (J) drip frame sides
2 pieces 32" long for (K) drip frame ends

¾" exterior-grade plywood
2 pieces 32"x92" for (C) base and (I) shelf

Hardware and miscellaneous
16 galvanized lag screws ½"x4½",
    washers
16d galvanized box nails
8d galvanized box nails
Staples
Tacks as needed
6-mil black plastic 4'x8' for drip catcher
4-mil black plastic as needed for lining
Rustproof screening (aluminum or
    fiberglass)
Wood preservative or stain (optional)

Ideas to Build On

Here are some ideas for adding on to the Putterer's Garden on page 30. The bed is designed to be used outdoors, but with some simple additions you can use it indoors during winter months or in cold climates. The bed can be modified in many ways so you can start seedlings, grow climbing plants, and more.

Pot Rack

If you live in an area where winters are too cold to keep plants in the bed outside, consider moving it into your basement or garage for part of the year. To make the heavy bed easier to move, you can build removable pot racks from pieces of plywood with legs attached, and keep soil mix in large separate containers. Then move the pots individually, along with the bed, outdoors when weather permits. Use ½-inch or thicker plywood for the rack.

Grow-light Frame

Many gardeners start plants from seed. You can get a head start even in a dark basement or garage by adding a simple frame to hold several fluorescent grow lights. Suspend lights on lengths of small chain from hooks screwed into the frame. You can raise lights as seedlings grow by shortening chains a few links at a time.

Most plants require very concentrated artificial light when grown indoors away from windows. Attach several frames to the bed, side by side, so that the entire area receives adequate light.

Greenhouse Cover

You can also extend the growing season by adding a greenhouse cover. Use this design as a starting point. Construction is simple. Just make two window frames of 1 by 3 lumber held together with L and T braces. Double-glaze them by

stapling heavy-gauge clear plastic to both sides. Nail frame together and attach the two window sections to frame with hinges. Tapering end pieces of frame allows water to run off the windows, but is unnecessary if you don't mind a little rain collecting on the plastic.

You may be able to simplify construction by using old wood-framed storm windows instead of building your own. You can also substitute screening for the glass or plastic to keep birds and bugs out during spring and summer.

Shade Cover

Some plants, especially seedlings, benefit from partial shade on hot summer days. Replace the greenhouse cover with a shade cover made of 2 by 2 lumber and lath. Nail 2 by 2s together with 8-penny (8d) galvanized box nails, and use 3d nails to attach lath. For 50 percent shade,

Pot Rack and Grow-light Frame

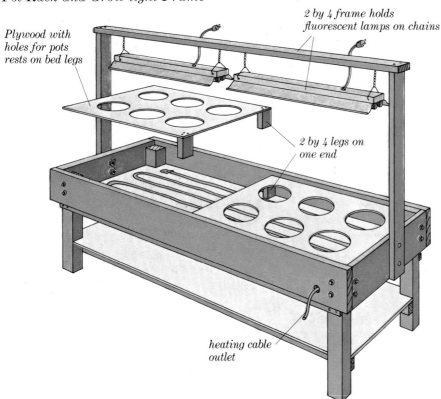

Plywood with holes for pots rests on bed legs

2 by 4 frame holds fluorescent lamps on chains

2 by 4 legs on one end

heating cable outlet

Simple Trellis

2 by 4 frame nailed to back of bed

strong cord or wire strung on screw eyes

make spaces between laths equal to width of lath. Make spaces wider or narrower to change the percentage.

Another way to make a shade cover is to replace the plastic on the greenhouse cover with the shade cloth used by nurseries. It is widely available in densities of 53 and 73 percent.

Simple Trellis

Other features can widen the range of uses for the Putterer's Garden. With the addition of a simple trellis, climbing plants or tomatoes have something to grab on to.

Heating Systems

Heating cables designed especially to keep soil warm can be buried in the base of the bed. Follow manufacturer's instructions for installing cables. Space cables evenly and make sure they do not cross.

Shade cover, made of lath strips, protects seedlings from too much sun. This cover is just one of many helpful items that can be added to the Putterer's Garden raised bed on page 30.

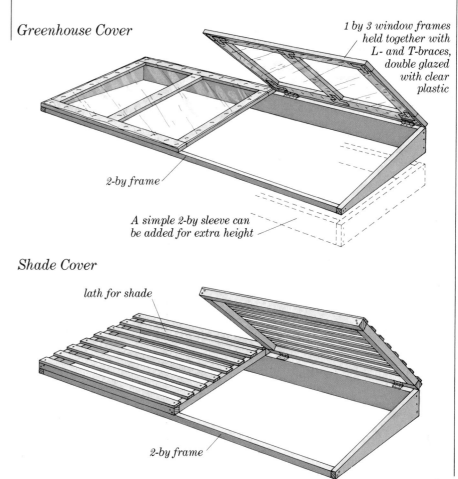

Greenhouse Cover

1 by 3 window frames held together with L- and T-braces, double glazed with clear plastic

2-by frame

A simple 2-by sleeve can be added for extra height

Shade Cover

lath for shade

2-by frame

33

The variety of trellis designs in this section is matched only by the many ways you can use them in landscaping your yard and garden. Trellises usually function as supports for vines and creeping plants, but they can also act as windbreaks or privacy screens, or stand as attractive wall decorations.

Trellises can be heavy or light, simple or complex. Some of the trellises in this section are freestanding units; others are designed with companion planter boxes for nurturing a climbing clematis or a healthy tomato harvest.

This ladder-style trellis made with standard dowels is an attractive variation on the more common lath trellises. Hardwood dowels ¾ inch in diameter, used in this design, will support over their 3-foot span just about any plant. Dowels from ⅛ inch to over 1 inch in diameter can be used, depending on the size and type of plants that will climb the trellis.

When the posts are attached to the overhang of a roof, they will support the trellis to a height of about 12 feet. Use 2 by 3 or 2 by 4 stock for the posts if you plan to make this trellis larger or freestanding.

When planning a customized trellis, keep in mind that most dowels come in 36-inch lengths. The most economical way to make a wider trellis is to join two or more sections made with 36-inch-long dowels (see detail illustration).

1. Begin construction by measuring distance from ground to rafters or soffit where you plan to attach trellis. Add a foot or so to this measurement to allow for sinking posts into ground, and cut posts (A) to length.

If you want trellis to be freestanding, instead of anchored to a building, make posts 2 feet longer than desired height of trellis. In either case, sharpen bottom of each post with a saw so you can drive it easily into ground.

2. Clamp posts together making sure ends are flush and lay out positions of dowel holes starting about 1½ feet from point where posts will enter ground. Mark a hole location every 8 inches and drill ¾-inch holes (or

With just standard dowels and two pieces of 2 by 2, you can turn a section of wall into a vertical flower bed.

holes for dowel size you have chosen). Drill through both posts at the same time to ensure that holes are in alignment. Work drill back and forth a couple of times in each hole to enlarge it just a bit—this will make it easier to insert the dowels.

3. Assemble trellis on a flat surface. Slide dowels through holes in one post, then work them into holes in the other. If rafters are spaced on 16-inch centers, outside edges of trellis posts should be 30½ inches apart to fit snugly against inside edges of the rafters. Check rafter spacing and adjust trellis if necessary. If you are building a freestanding trellis, use any convenient spacing.

4. Once you've determined the distance needed between posts, nail each dowel end into post with a 4-penny (4d) galvanized finishing nail. In order to prevent the hardwood dowels from splitting, first drill pilot holes with a $\frac{1}{16}$-inch drill bit through posts into dowels.

5. Thoroughly coat bottom ends of posts (or entire trellis, if desired) with wood preservative. See page 8 for information on preservatives.

6. Mark points where trellis will be attached to rafters. Hang a plumb bob (or a weighted piece of string) from these points to ground and mark positions on ground. Drill a ¼-inch hole through each post about 2 inches from top, and through rafters where you marked them. Place pointed ends of posts in marks on ground and push them into ground the desired distance (or have a helper hammer on tops of posts). Line up holes in posts and rafters and insert carriage bolts.

If roof has an enclosed soffit that prevents attaching posts directly to rafters, use large corner braces. Screw these braces to posts and to bottom of soffit.

If trellis is freestanding, just push or hammer posts into ground about 2 feet. Hold trellis plumb and tamp soil firmly to anchor it securely. If ground is too hard or there is a hardpan, dig holes with a post-hole digger, set posts, backfill with dirt, and tamp ground firmly with a shovel handle or similar implement.

Materials List

2x2 rough redwood
2 pieces approximately 12' long for (A) posts

¾" dia hardwood dowel
14 pieces 36" long for (B) dowels

Hardware and miscellaneous
4d galvanized finishing nails
2 galvanized carriage bolts ¼"x3½", washers, wing nuts
Plated corner braces if needed
Wood preservative

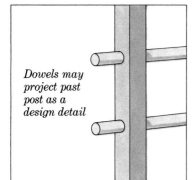

Dowels may project past post as a design detail

For a wider trellis, join 2 sets of dowels at a post

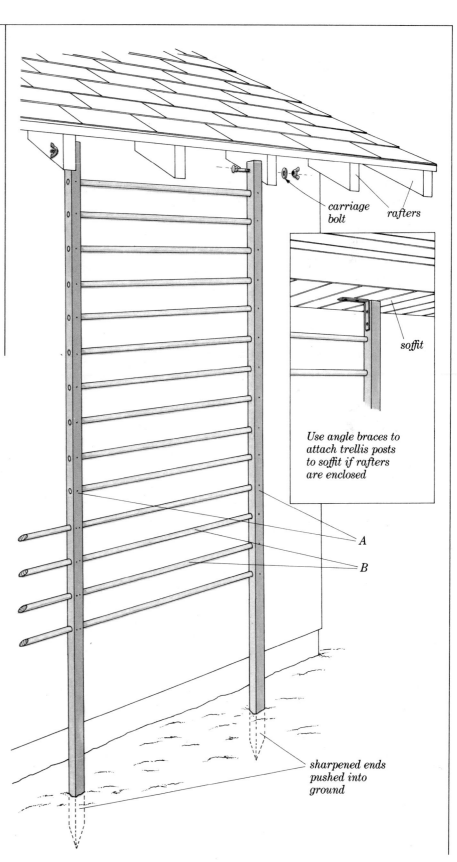

carriage bolt

rafters

soffit

Use angle braces to attach trellis posts to soffit if rafters are enclosed

A

B

sharpened ends pushed into ground

35

A-frame Trellis

This freestanding trellis is versatile and very easy to make. A simple hinge arrangement at the top allows you to adjust the trellis to the exact span and height needed to support a wide variety of plants. Since it is freestanding, it can be used to support vine plants sowed directly into the ground, or you can build the companion planter boxes and straddle them with the trellis.

Another option is to open the "A" completely and create a straight vertical trellis that can be hung on a wall or suspended from the edge of a roof.

1. Cut legs (A) and slats (B).

2. Assemble sides by nailing horizontal slats to legs, then nailing vertical slats in place. Use two 3-penny (3d) galvanized box nails at each joint. Using waterproof glue in addition to nails will make a stronger joint.

Nail topmost slat to ends of legs first. Then cut two 6-inch lengths of scrap 1 by 2 and place them along legs so they butt tightly against top slat. Place next horizontal slat against these spacers and nail it to legs. Follow procedure to attach all slats.

3. Turn trellis over and install vertical slats in the same way, working across from one leg to the other.

4. When both halves are assembled, place them face down on a flat surface with tops together and sides flush. Install hinges, positioning them so that the mounting screws will penetrate first vertical slat inside legs. If hinges come with screws that are shorter than 1½ inches, replace them with longer screws (these will hold top of trellis together where most of stress is concentrated).

Designed for growing vine crops vertically, this A-frame Trellis has lemon cucumbers on one side and beans on the other. The trellis is a separate unit that can be used with a variety of containers.

Materials List

1x2 rough redwood
4 pieces 72" long for (A) legs
28 pieces 54" long for (B) slats

Hardware and miscellaneous
3d galvanized box nails
2 brass butt hinges 1½", with screws
Waterproof glue (optional)

Trellis Planter Boxes

1. Cut sides (C) and ends (D) and nail them together with 8d galvanized box nails.

2. Cut base (E) so that it fits in box formed by sides and ends. Drill drainage holes and cover them by tacking on rustproof screening. Cut legs (H), place them flush with corners of base, and nail in place through base. Nail base in place through sides and ends.

3. Cut side and end caps (F and G).

Miter ends at 45 degrees so they fit exactly flush with inside of box. Nail them in place. Drive an additional nail horizontally through mitered joint to lock corners together.

4. Fill boxes with soil mix, plant seeds, and set trellis in place as shown in photographs.

Materials List
Two planter boxes

1x8 rough redwood
4 pieces 48" long for (C) sides
4 pieces 10½" long for (D) ends

¾" exterior-grade plywood
2 pieces 10½"x46" for (E) base

4x4 rough redwood
8 pieces 4" long for (H) legs

1x2 rough redwood
4 pieces 50" long for (F) side caps
4 pieces 14½" long for (G) end caps

Hardware and miscellaneous
8d galvanized box nails
Tacks as needed
Rustproof screening (aluminum or fiberglass)

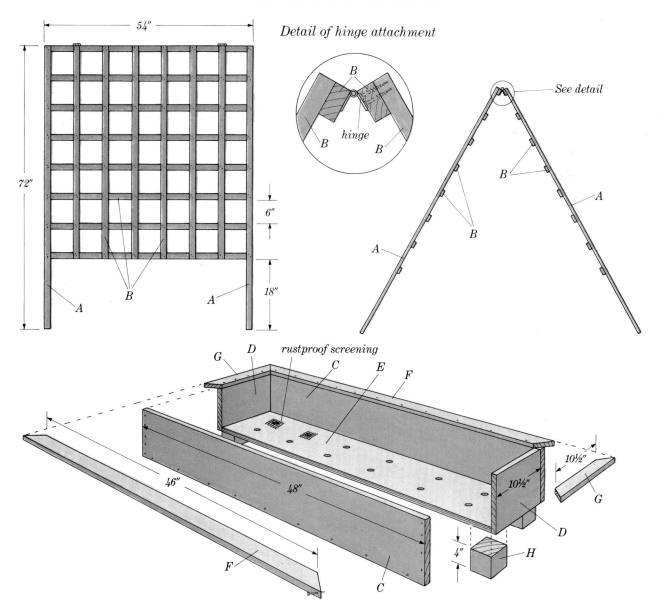

Detail of hinge attachment

Espalier Trellis

This project includes two types of trellises, both of which can be attached to a basic planter box. One is designed to support grape vines strung over sturdy wire. The other supports the lateral branches of an apple tree. If you prune the tree judiciously, the trunk will follow the center vertical while selected branches can be trained along the horizontals.

Either design allows two or more planter boxes to share one trellis assembly. Place grape boxes end-to-end and share the center upright. Place two apple boxes back-to-back and grow two trees on one trellis.

Fruit trees and vines can be grown in small yards or on patios with the Grape Trellis (top) and Apple Trellis (above) and the companion planter box.

Trellis Planter Box

1. Cut sides (A), ends (B), corner posts (D), and feet (E).

2. Nail ends to corner posts with 8-penny (8d) galvanized box nails. Tops of posts should be flush with tops of ends. Next, nail side boards to end assemblies with 8d nails through sides and ends. Keep assembly square as you nail.

3. Turn assembly over, and measure and cut base (C) to size. Drill ½-inch drainage holes and tack rustproof screening over them. Glue and nail feet to base so that they protrude 1½ inches at sides and ends. Nail base in place through sides.

Grape Trellis

1. Cut uprights (T1) and cross arms (T2). You may want to bevel or round corners for a more finished look.

2. Center a cross arm at top of each upright and attach with two ¼-inch lag screws. Drill ³⁄₁₆-inch pilot holes through cross arms and into uprights for lag screws. Follow same procedure to install lower arms 16 inches below upper arms. Use a framing square to check that arms and uprights meet at right angles.

3. Place planter box on level ground. Hold one upright against end of box so it is flush with bottom of box and centered. Drill a ³⁄₈-inch hole through upright into end and insert a ³⁄₈-inch carriage bolt. Use a carpenter's level to check that upright is plumb. Hold it in place, drill second bolt hole, and insert bolt. Secure bolts with hex nuts, or use wing nuts for easy removal of the trellis. Install other upright assembly in the same way.

4. Trellis wires run from large screw eyes in one cross member to eye bolts in the other. Drill ⅛-inch pilot holes for screw eyes and ¼-inch holes for eye bolts. Insert screw eyes, twist wires around them, and stretch wires to loosely attached eye bolts. Twist wires around eye bolts. Tighten wing nuts to put tension in wires.

Apple Trellis

1. Cut uprights (T3) and slats (T4).

2. Place 2 outer uprights on a flat surface so that their outer edges are 48 inches apart. Center top slat over uprights and nail it in place with 8d box or finishing nails. Check that uprights remain parallel. Nail next slat in place 11 inches below the first, then attach remaining slats.

3. Attach center upright to slats. When trellis is complete, use two ¼-inch lag screws per upright to attach trellis to back of planter box. Drill ³⁄₁₆-inch pilot holes for screws. Use shorter screws in center upright.

Materials List

Trellis Planter Box

2x10 surfaced redwood
4 pieces 48" long for (A) sides
4 pieces 12" long for (B) ends

2x4 surfaced redwood
4 pieces 17¾" long for (D) corner posts

4x4 surfaced redwood
4 pieces 5" long for (E) feet

¾" exterior-grade plywood
1 piece 12"x45" for (C) base

Hardware and miscellaneous
8d galvanized box nails
Tacks as needed
Rustproof screening (aluminum or fiberglass)
Waterproof glue

Grape Trellis

2x4 surfaced redwood
2 pieces 60" long for (T1) uprights
4 pieces 18" long for (T2) cross arms

Hardware and miscellaneous
8 lag screws ¼"x2½"
4 carriage bolts ³⁄₈"x3½", washers, hex nuts or wing nuts
4 large screw eyes
4 eye bolts ¼"x3", washers, wing nuts
20' aluminum clothesline or aluminum or copper wire

Apple Trellis

2x4 surfaced redwood
3 pieces 62" long for (T3) uprights
4 pieces 60" long for (T4) slats

Hardware and miscellaneous
8d galvanized box or finishing nails
2 lag screws ¼"x2½", washers
4 lag screws ¼"x3½", washers

Espalier Trellis Planter Box

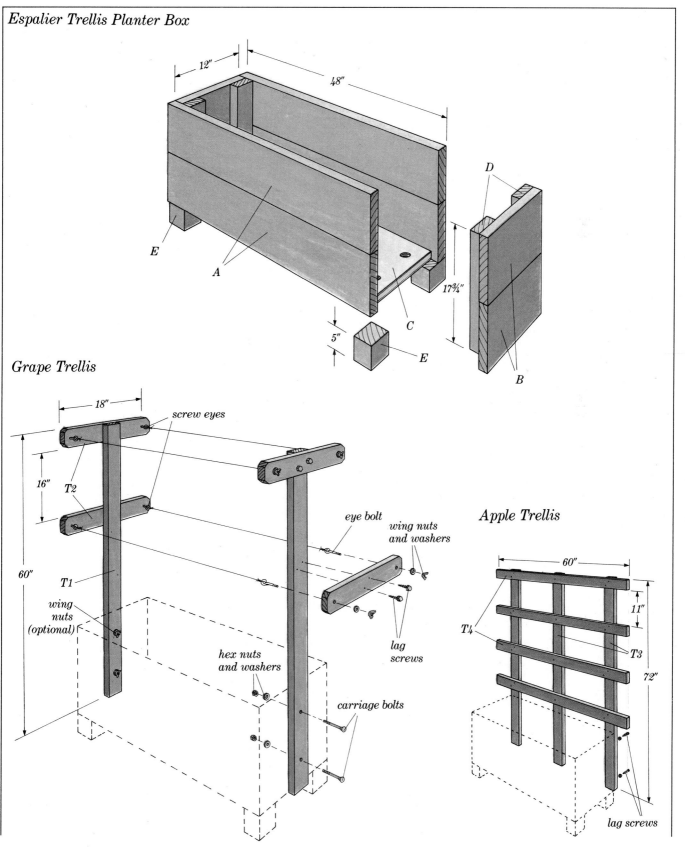

12"

48"

D

17¾"

E

A

C

5"

E

B

Grape Trellis

18"

screw eyes

16"

T2

60"

T1

wing
nuts
(optional)

hex nuts
and washers

carriage bolts

eye bolt

wing nuts
and washers

lag
screws

Apple Trellis

60"

11"

T4

T3

72"

lag screws

Vegetable Trellis

Cucumbers and other vegetables, as well as tomatoes, grow well in this sturdy planter/trellis combination. The vertical trellis posts form part of the box back to make an integrated unit.

This trellis design incorporates a basic planter box with lengthened back members that form the vertical posts of the trellis. As a self-contained unit, it has added strength and stability and is ideal for a crop of heavy vegetables.

The cross members can be either set in notches cut in the vertical posts or simply nailed to the verticals. We've supplied instructions for both designs; either one will give you an attractive, rugged trellis.

1. Cut planter box slats (A), front leg posts (B), and trellis posts (F). Cut side cleats (D) and front and back cleats (E). For simpler trellis, cut cross members (G1) from 1 by 2 stock; for notched trellis, cut cross members (G2) from 2 by 2 stock.

2. Assemble planter front first. Lay 9 slats on a flat surface and nail and glue 2 front cleats to them with 6-penny (6d) galvanized finishing nails. Use 2 nails per slat and stagger nails to prevent splitting cleat. Top cleat should be flush with top of slats, and bottom cleat should be ¾ inch up from bottom of slats.

3. Attach front leg posts to outsides of front assembly with 3 No. 14 flat-head wood screws per post. Drill ⅛-inch pilot holes for screws to avoid splitting wood.

4. Make back in the same way, but use a trellis post for the center slat. If you decide to notch trellis posts to receive cross members, cut notches in all 3 trellis posts at the same time before they are installed, as follows.

Clamp posts together and lay out the 5 notches on all 3 posts at once. Make a saw cut at each edge of the 1½-inch-wide by ¾-inch deep notch and several in between. Remove wood with a sharp chisel. Notches can also be cut with a table or radial-arm saw with a dado attachment.

5. Position the 2 outer trellis posts at ends of planter back so they extend 3 inches below bottom of slats, and attach them to slats with 3 No. 14 flat-head wood screws per post. Drill pilot holes for the screws.

6. Assemble sides as you did front. Note that each side cleat is set ¾ inch from outside edges of end slats to allow room for front and back cleats when sides are brought together. Join sides to back with 3 No. 14 flat-head wood screws per side, then attach front in the same way.

7. Measure and cut plywood base (C) to fit exactly into square formed by sides. Drill four or five ½-inch drainage holes in base and cover by tacking on rustproof screening. Nail base in place below cleats with 6d nails through sides.

8. Tip assembly back so trellis posts lie on a flat surface. To install simple trellis cross members, center first cross member on posts 3 inches from top and nail it in place with six 6d nails. Cut 2 pieces of scrap 9½ inches long and use them as spacers as you nail on remaining cross members.

For notched trellis, install cross members by centering them in notches cut in posts. Secure each with three 6d nails.

Materials List

2x2 surfaced redwood
35 pieces 12″ long for (A) slats
2 pieces 15″ long for (B) front leg post
3 pieces 72″ long for (F) trellis posts
5 pieces 22½″ long for (G2) cross members

1x2 surfaced redwood
4 pieces 12″ long for (D) side cleats
4 pieces 13½″ long for (E) front and back cleats
5 pieces 22½″ long for (G1) cross members

¾″ exterior-grade plywood
1 piece 13½″x13½″ for (C) base

Hardware and miscellaneous
6d galvanized finishing nails
24 flat-head wood screws 2¾″x#14
Tacks as needed
Rustproof screening (aluminum or fiberglass)

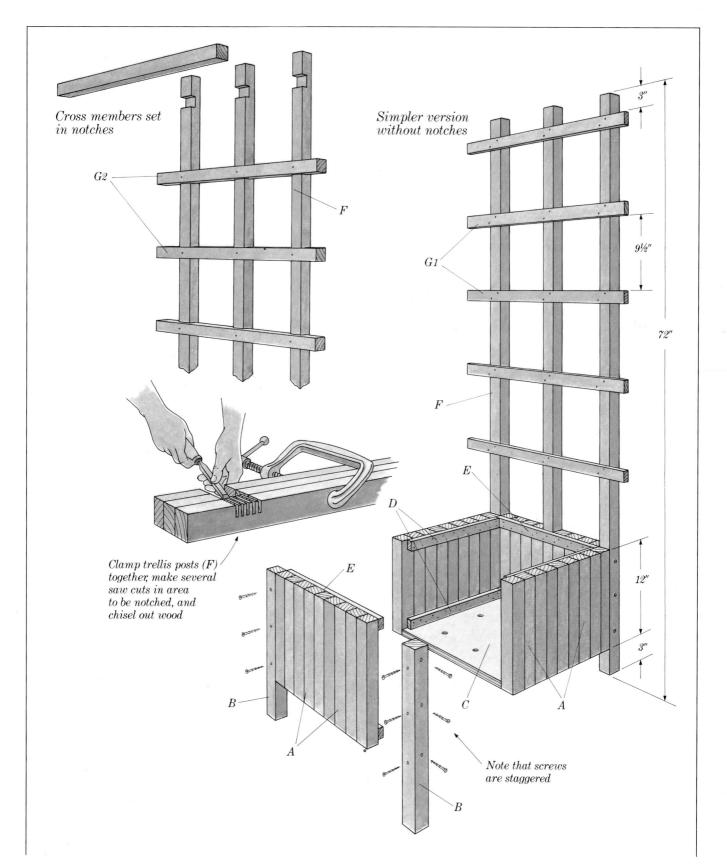

Cross members set in notches

G2

F

Simpler version without notches

3"

G1

9½"

72"

F

E

D

12"

E

3"

Clamp trellis posts (F) together, make several saw cuts in area to be notched, and chisel out wood

B

A

B

A

C

A

Note that screws are staggered

Melon Trellis

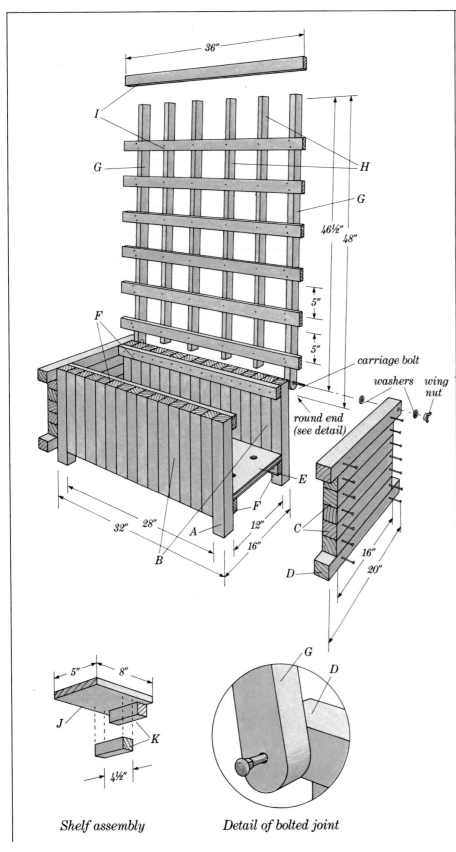

36"

I

G

H

G

46½"

48"

5"

5"

carriage bolt

washers   wing nut

round end
(see detail)

F

E

F

A

B

32"   28"   12"   16"

C

D   16"

20"

G   D

5"   8"

J

K

4½"

Shelf assembly   *Detail of bolted joint*

This planter box and its sturdy, adjustable trellis are specially designed to provide adequate support for the vines and fruit of watermelons, but may be used for other vine crops such as squash and cantaloupes. The movable shelves slide over the trellis slats and can be placed wherever the plant produces a melon.

1. Cut legs (A), sides (B), ends (C), rails (D), and shelf cleats (K). Cut side cleats (F), trellis supports (G), trellis rails (H), and trellis slats (I).

2. On a flat surface, glue and nail side cleats to side pieces. Line up 14 side pieces and place a leg at each end. Using 6-penny (6d) galvanized box nails, attach upper cleat flush with top edges of side pieces and lower cleat flush with bottom of side pieces. For a stronger box, glue side pieces and legs together before nailing on cleats.

3. Glue and nail rails (D) and end pieces (C) to legs of assembled sides with 16d galvanized box nails. Begin at one end by nailing a rail in place flush with tops of sides. Then glue and nail on end pieces, working from top down. Drill pilot holes for nails near ends of rails and end pieces to prevent wood from splitting.

4. When one end is complete, measure and cut base (E) to fit. Drill ½-inch drainage holes and tack rust-proof screening over them. Nail base in place with 6d nails through sides. Then attach other end of box as you did first.

5. Using a saw or wood rasp, bevel or round corners of bottom ends of trellis supports (G). Drill ¼-inch holes for carriage bolts centered in ends of upper rails (D) and in beveled ends of trellis supports. Bolt trellis supports to insides of rails with ¼-inch by 3½-inch carriage bolts and wing nuts.

6. Now turn box on its back so trellis supports are on floor. Glue and nail top slat (I) so it is flush with top of trellis supports and overhangs equally on each end. Use two 6d box nails per joint. Check that supports are same distance apart at the top as

they are at the bottom. Cut two 5-inch pieces of scrap to use as temporary spacers while you glue and nail remaining slats to supports.

7. Next, nail trellis rails (H) in place with 6d nails. Start at one side and space them approximately 5 inches apart. You may have to adjust spacing of center rails by eye.

8. Turn planter box right side up and swing trellis unit upright. Tighten wing nuts to hold trellis up. For a freestanding trellis, cut additional supports from 1 by 2 stock. Bolt these pieces to trellis supports (G) with short, ¼-inch by 2-inch carriage bolts so that additional supports hang from trellis to ground, supporting trellis at a convenient angle.

9. Make melon shelves (J) by cutting 5-inch lengths of 1 by 8 stock and nailing a shelf cleat to bottom of each, flush with back edge. Drive 6d nails through shelf into cleat. Then, using a piece of 1 by 2 as a spacer, nail on second cleat. Space between cleats should be just large enough for trellis slat to fit.

Materials List

2x2 rough redwood
4 pieces 16″ long for (A) legs
28 pieces 14″ long for (B) sides
10 pieces 16″ long for (C) ends
4 pieces 20″ long for (D) rails
8 pieces 4½″ long for (K) shelf cleats

1x2 rough redwood
4 pieces 32″ long for (F) side cleats
2 pieces 48″ long for (G) trellis supports
4 pieces 46½″ long for (H) trellis rails
7 pieces 36″ long for (I) trellis slats

¾″ exterior-grade plywood
1 piece 12″x32″ for (E) base

1x8 rough redwood
4 pieces 5″ long for (J) shelves (makes
    4 shelves)

Hardware and miscellaneous
6d galvanized box nails
16d galvanized box nails
2 carriage bolts ¼″x3½″, 4 washers,
    2 wing nuts
2 carriage bolts ¼″x2″, washers, wing
    nuts (for optional supports for a free-
    standing trellis)
Waterproof glue
Tacks as needed
Rustproof screening (aluminum or
    fiberglass)

Above. *This trellis pivots on bolts and can be adjusted to lean at whatever angle is most convenient for a specific location or type of plant.*
Left. *Movable shelves fit over trellis crosspieces to support fruits or vegetables.*

Folding Trellis

The Folding Trellis is the most adaptable of the trellises shown in this section. It works like an accordion, so its height and width can be adjusted for various situations. It can be used with any type of planter box or pots. Being collapsible, the trellis is easily transported anywhere in the garden and stores compactly at the end of the growing season.

This trellis is designed to support small- to medium-sized plants. If you need a longer trellis, build several and connect them.

1. Begin construction by cutting post halves (A), top fillers (B), bottom fillers (C), and slats (D, E, F, and G).

2. Nail post halves to top and bottom fillers with 4-penny (4d) galvanized box nails. Cut bottom end of each post to a point so it will be easy to push into ground.

3. Layout and drilling of the pivot holes are the most critical phases of this project. These holes must be accurately spaced for trellis to open and close smoothly. Holes in all slats and posts are the same size.

Mark and drill all holes in 1 long slat (D). Drill one ⅛-inch hole ¾ inch from each end, another in the exact center of the slat, and 2 more evenly spaced between center hole and each end hole. If you use slat dimensions given above, all holes will be 8 inches apart.

Use this slat as a pattern for drilling all remaining slats. Stack and clamp several together so you can drill them at once. Be sure to keep drill perpendicular to slats as you work. Drill shorter slats by placing one end flush with end of pattern slat.

4. When all ⅛-inch holes are drilled, enlarge one end hole in each of the (E), (F), and (G) slats to ¼ inch. These holes are for the carriage bolts that attach trellis to posts.

5. Begin assembly by temporarily bolting 2 (F) slats together at their ends with a carriage bolt. Place slats on a flat surface and arrange them so they form a 90-degree angle. Next, place an (E) slat on top of bottom (F) slat as shown in the illustration.

Attach the 2 slats at the first ⅛-inch-diameter hole on each by slipping a washer over a cotter pin and inserting pin through both slats. Then slip another washer on cotter pin and bend pin open.

Turn slats over and install another (E) slat perpendicular to first by fastening it to the (F) slat at the first hole and to the first (E) slat (installed on other side) at the second hole where they cross. Make sure you insert all cotter pins from the same side. Install a (D) slat next; it crosses both the (E) and (F) slats. Turn trellis over and install another (D) slat. A careful look at the illustration makes this a simple procedure.

Install the 4 short (G) slats on ends of (E) and (F) slats. Note that a cotter pin is used in joint between each (G) and (D) slat and a carriage bolt in joint of (G) and (E). Fasten remaining (D) slats, then complete other end.

6. When trellis is complete, open and close it to test for free movement. If there is a binding joint, remove cotter pin and enlarge hole. When trellis moves smoothly, tighten joints by hitting cotter pin arms with a hammer to flatten them tightly against washers.

7. Attach posts to trellis with carriage bolts. Place 3 washers between trellis and post and 1 washer between post and wing nut. Adjust final width of trellis, then tighten wing nuts and push posts into ground.

Materials List

1x2 surfaced redwood
4 pieces 72″ long for (A) post halves

¼ x1½ redwood lath
2 pieces 4″ long for (B) top fillers
2 pieces 18″ long for (C) bottom fillers
8 pieces 49½″ long for (D) slats
4 pieces 41½″ long for (E) slats
4 pieces 25½″ long for (F) slats
4 pieces 9½″ long for (G) slats

Hardware and miscellaneous
4d galvanized box nails
46 cotter pins ⅛″x1¼″
92 washers ⅛″
6 carriage bolts ¼″x2″, wing nuts
24 washers ¼″

This versatile, adjustable-width trellis can be anchored in the ground, used freestanding as a screen, or attached to a wall or the back of a large planter box.

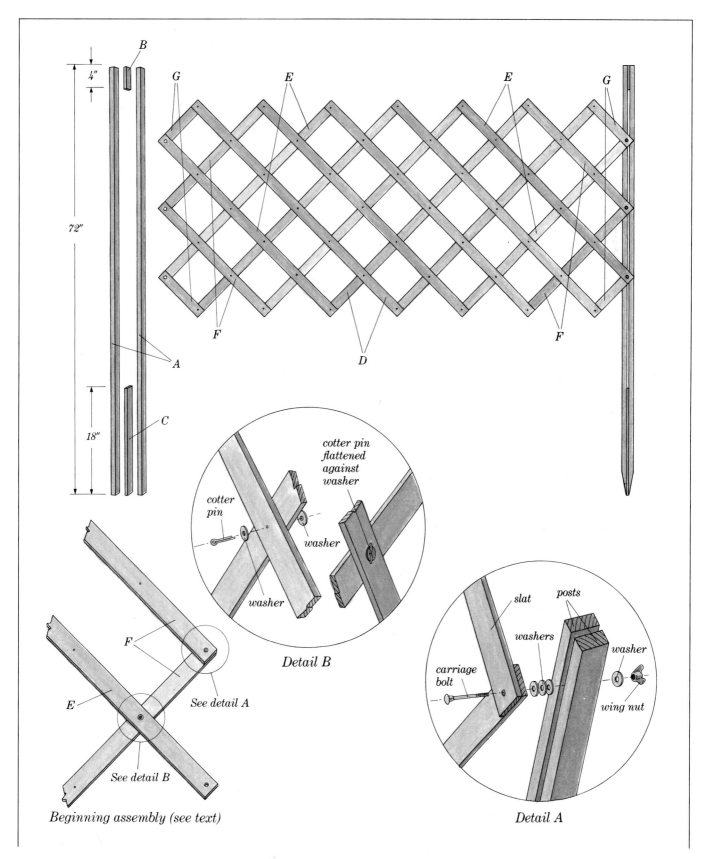

4"

B

72"

G

E

E

G

A

18"

C

F

D

F

cotter pin
flattened
against
washer

cotter
pin

washer

washer

Detail B

slat

posts

washers

carriage
bolt

washer

wing nut

Detail A

F

E

See detail A

See detail B

Beginning assembly (see text)

Corner Trellis

This handsome container is ideally suited for vine crops. The planter box has sloping, mitered sides that require a compound-angle saw cut. This is not a difficult cut for an experienced woodworker, but you might want to wait until you have completed some of the easier projects before you tackle this one. A table or radial-arm saw will help, but is not necessary; all cuts can be made with a straightedge and a circular saw that has a blade-angle adjustment.

1. Cut sides (A) and (B) to their rough sizes, about 34 and 26 inches, respectively. Cut corner posts (D), trellis uprights (F), 3 lengths of trellis slats (G, H, and I), and feet (E).

2. Making compound cuts is not difficult if you take time in the layout. The quickest way to make them without a table or radial-arm saw is to lay 2 side pieces (A) and (B) in position, centered, on a piece of scrap plywood and tack them in place (see illustration). Mark center and from it lay out the 30-inch top dimension and the 14-inch bottom dimension. Connect marks with a straightedge and, using a protractor, check that lines form a 20-degree angle to a vertical line.

3. Set saw blade to a 42-degree angle. Carefully measure distance from blade to edge of base plate of saw. Then tack a straight-edged cleat to boards that distance from cut line; cleat will guide saw. Check that you are cutting the angle correctly; layout is for outside dimensions of planter, so cut with blade tilted toward undersides of boards as in the illustration. Follow these same steps to cut remaining 3 sides of planter.

4. Assemble 2 of the sides by attaching corner posts (D) so they are flush with inside of miter cut. Use 8-penny (8d) galvanized box nails. Be sure to allow ¾ inch clearance at bottom for base. Nail one (A) piece and one (B) piece to these assembled sides with 8d nails to form a third side.

5. Next, measure and cut base (C) to fit. Set saw at 20 degrees when you cut base so its edges will fit snugly against sides. Drill four ½-inch drainage holes in base and tack rustproof screening over them. Position feet flush with corners of base and nail them in place with 8d nails through base. Then slide base into place within the 3 assembled sides and attach with 8d nails through sides. It may be helpful to drill pilot holes first so the nails will be driven in horizontally. Finally, nail on remaining side pieces to complete box.

6. Installing trellis is easy. Place uprights (F) in position, approximately 1 inch in from edge of planter box, and drill two ³/₁₆-inch pilot holes through each into side of planter box as shown in illustration. Remove uprights and enlarge holes in them to ¼ inch. Replace uprights and insert lag screws and washers.

7. Lay planter on its back so 2 uprights are on the ground, and nail top trellis slat flush with tops of uprights. Use 8d nails. Nail remaining slats in place, spaced 15¾ inches apart. Cut ends of slats flush with uprights.

Make the unnoticed corner of a patio into a focal point with this trellis, or place it at the edge of a patio or deck to define the space.

Materials List

2x12 rough redwood
4 pieces 34″ long for (A) sides
4 pieces 26″ long for (B) sides

2x4 rough redwood
4 pieces 20″ long for (D) corner posts
4 pieces 72″ long for (F) trellis uprights

1x4 rough redwood
2 pieces 63″ long for (G) slats
2 pieces 52″ long for (H) slats
2 pieces 41″ long for (I) slats

4x4 rough redwood
4 pieces 4″ long for (E) feet

¾″ exterior-grade plywood
1 piece approx 12″x12″ for (C) base

Hardware and miscellaneous
8d galvanized box nails
8 lag screws ¼″x3½″, washers
Tacks as needed
Rustproof screening (aluminum or fiberglass)

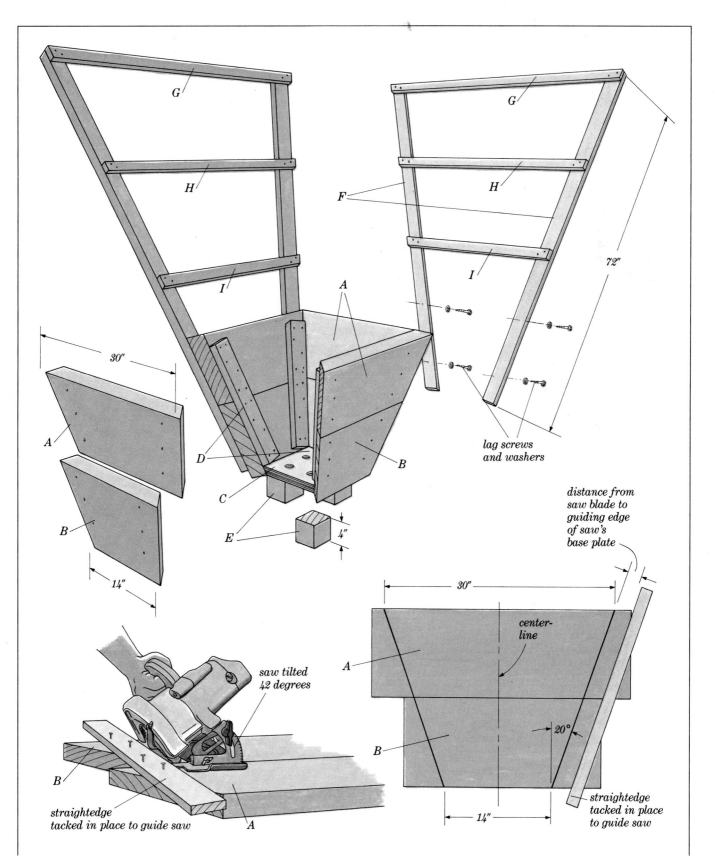

G

F

H

I

A

A

B

D

C

E

30"

14"

4"

72"

lag screws
and washers

distance from
saw blade to
guiding edge
of saw's
base plate

saw tilted
42 degrees

B

straightedge
tacked in place to guide saw

A

30"

A

center-
line

14"

20°

B

straightedge
tacked in place
to guide saw

Decorative Screen Trellis

This beautiful screen is really more of a
garden decoration than a trellis. The
detailed edging of the top rail and
half-lap joinery give it a
distinctive appearance.

This handsome three-panel trellis
can act as a screen to create a
lovely backdrop for your garden or
patio. Construction is straightforward,
although somewhat more technical
than for most of our other trellises.

1. Begin by cutting horizontal slats
(A), vertical slats (B), sides (C), and
top rails (D).

2. All joints in this trellis are half-lap.
The easiest method of cutting joints is
with a radial-arm or table saw
equipped with a dado blade. Set saw
to make a ¾-inch-deep cut and adjust
dado blade to its widest setting.

Lay out and cut dadoes in sides
first. Pair up pieces and carefully
align their ends. First cut 3½-inch-
wide dado for top rails in both boards
at once, then cut the eight 1½-inch-
wide dadoes for slats.

3. Use one of the sides as a pattern
when laying out dadoes in vertical
slats (B). Clamp slats together and cut
1½-inch-wide dadoes for horizontal
slats in both at the same time.

4. Lay out and cut dadoes in horizontal slats next. Cut 3½-inch-wide

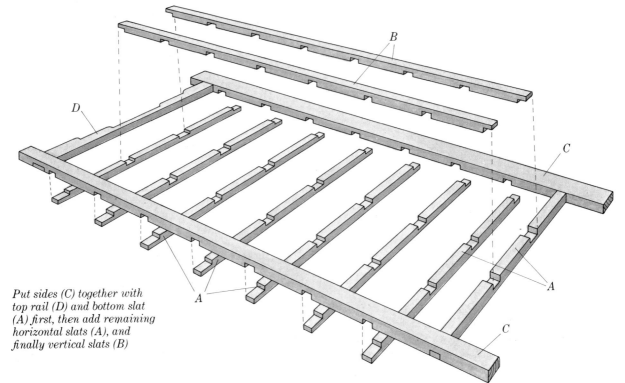

Put sides (C) together with
top rail (D) and bottom slat
(A) first, then add remaining
horizontal slats (A), and
finally vertical slats (B)

dadoes at slat ends for sides, and 1½-inch-wide dadoes in center for vertical slats.

5. Enlarge pattern for top rail by drawing a grid of ½-inch squares and copying pattern, then transfer pattern to one of the top pieces. Cut decorative edge with a saber or coping saw, then use this piece as a pattern when cutting other 2 top rails. Cut a 3½-inch-wide dado on both ends of each top rail.

6. Assemble each of the 3 trellis panels by gluing and nailing top rail and lowest horizontal slat to sides with waterproof glue and galvanized ring-shank nails. Drive nails through horizontal slats into side pieces. Check that all parts are square, then install

remaining horizontal slats with glue and nails.

7. Next, apply glue to joints of horizontal and vertical slats and nail in verticals. Assemble other 2 panels in the same way.

8. When glue is dry, chip away excess with a sharp chisel (it comes off better this way than by wiping it when it's wet). Then use a router equipped with a chamfer bit to cut a ⅛-inch bevel on all edges of each side piece. If you don't have a router, round edges with abrasive paper.

9. Stack the 3 finished panels as shown in illustration. Install 3 bifold hinges on each side in the positions illustrated. Check hinge action; you should be able to fold panels in either

direction. Remember when you erect trellis that panels should meet at an angle close to 90 degrees to prevent trellis from falling in a high wind or under an unbalanced load.

Materials List

2x2 surfaced redwood
24 pieces 32½" long for (A) horizontal slats
6 pieces 57½" long for (B) vertical slats

2x4 surfaced redwood
6 pieces 71½" long for (C) sides
3 pieces 32½" long for (D) top rails

Hardware and miscellaneous
Galvanized ring-shank nails 1⅜"
6 (3 pairs) bifold hinges with screws
Waterproof glue

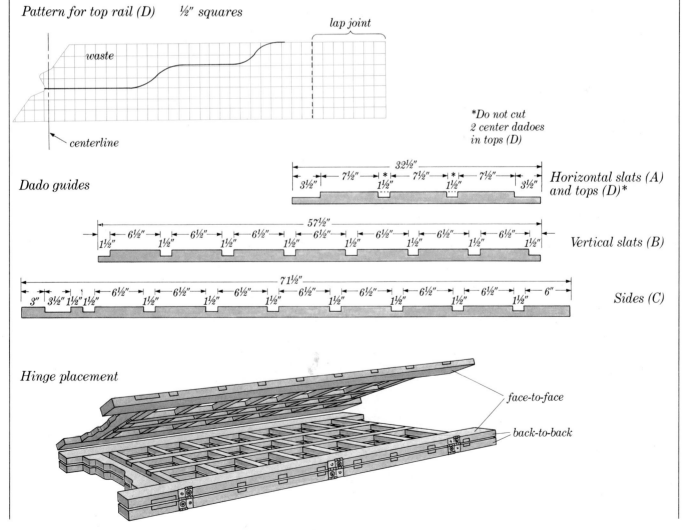

Pattern for top rail (D)   ½" squares

lap joint

waste

centerline

*Do not cut
2 center dadoes
in tops (D)

Dado guides

32½"
3½" — 7½" — * — 7½" — * — 7½" — 3½"
1½"   1½"

Horizontal slats (A) and tops (D)*

57½"
1½" — 6½" — 1½" — 6½" — 1½" — 6½" — 1½" — 6½" — 1½" — 6½" — 1½" — 6½" — 1½"

Vertical slats (B)

71½"
3" — 3½" 1½" 1½" — 6½" — 1½" — 6½" — 1½" — 6½" — 1½" — 6½" — 1½" — 6½" — 1½" — 6½" — 1½" — 6"

Sides (C)

Hinge placement

face-to-face

back-to-back

Sunburst Trellis

In season, these whimsical Sunburst Trellises enhance their plantings; in dormant months they are attractive elements on their own.

Materials List

1x2 surfaced redwood
4 pieces 36″ long for (F) and (G) frame
2 pieces 52″ long for (J) side supports
1 piece 37½″ long for (K) top support

1x12 surfaced pine
1 piece 11¼″ long for (H) sun

1x1 pine trim
9 pieces 42″ long for (I) sun rays

Hardware and miscellaneous
8d galvanized finishing nails
3d galvanized finishing nails
4 flat-head brass wood screws 2″x#14
9 Scotch fasteners
Abrasive paper as needed
Waterproof glue

The Sunburst Trellis is both decorative and functional. Construct two trellises, each placed atop a planter, and together they form an attractive support for plants.

You can also build the trellis alone and hang it on a wall or fence, or make the trellis freestanding by lengthening the side frame members and anchoring them in the ground. The quantities in the Materials List make one trellis and planter box.

1. Cut horizontal and vertical frame pieces (F) and (G), side supports (J), and top support (K). For the sun (H), trace an arc with an 11¼-inch radius on 1 by 12 stock, and cut with a coping saw or electric saber saw. Cut the 9 sun rays (I) from 1 by 1 trim stock. (Sun rays can also be ripped from 1 by 12 or 1 by 2 stock.)

2. Lay out frame pieces on a flat surface to form a square. Observe the configuration of ends in the detail illustration. Drill two 1/16-inch pilot holes through ends of horizontal frame pieces (F) to prevent wood from splitting. Locate first hole ½ inch from end and the second hole 1 inch from the same end. Nail horizontals (F) to verticals (G) with 8-penny (8d) galvanized finishing nails.

3. Place sun in one lower corner of frame, flush with outside edges, and nail it to frame with 3d galvanized finishing nails.

4. Lay frame on a flat surface and place a scrap of ¾-inch stock under rounded edge of sun for support while installing rays. With abrasive paper, put a slight concave curve on ends of rays where they will fit against edge of sun.

5. Locate position of first ray by stretching a string from corner of frame that is covered by the sun to opposite corner. Use 3d nails to attach ray to corner, and a Scotch fastener to attach it to sun. Using waterproof glue in addition will make this joint more secure.

6. Space other rays evenly around sun. Attach rays and cut them all flush with outside edges of frame. Nail side supports (J) to frame with 3d nails, then install top support (K).

7. After building planter box, attach each trellis side support to ends of box with 2 No. 14 flat-head brass wood screws. Make ⅛-inch pilot holes before installing screws.

Trellis Planter Box

1. Cut sides (A), ends (B), corner cleats (D), and feet (E).

2. Make ⅛-inch staggered pilot holes through corner cleats and screw cleats to ends with 3″ by No. 14 screws. Cleats should be 2 inches up from bottom to allow room for base. Assemble box by again making pilot holes and screwing sides to cleats.

3. Cut base (C) to fit inside box. Drill ½-inch drainage holes and cover them with rustproof screening. Then screw each foot to base with 3 No. 14 screws. Nail base to sides and ends with 16d galvanized finishing nails.

Materials List

2x12 rough redwood
2 pieces 36″ long for (A) sides
2 pieces 12″ long for (B) ends
1 piece 32″ long for (C) base

2x2 rough redwood
4 pieces 9″ long for (D) corner cleats
2 pieces 11″ long for (E) feet

Hardware and miscellaneous
16d galvanized finishing nails
30 flat-head brass wood screws 3″x#14
Rustproof screening (aluminum or fiberglass)
Tacks as needed

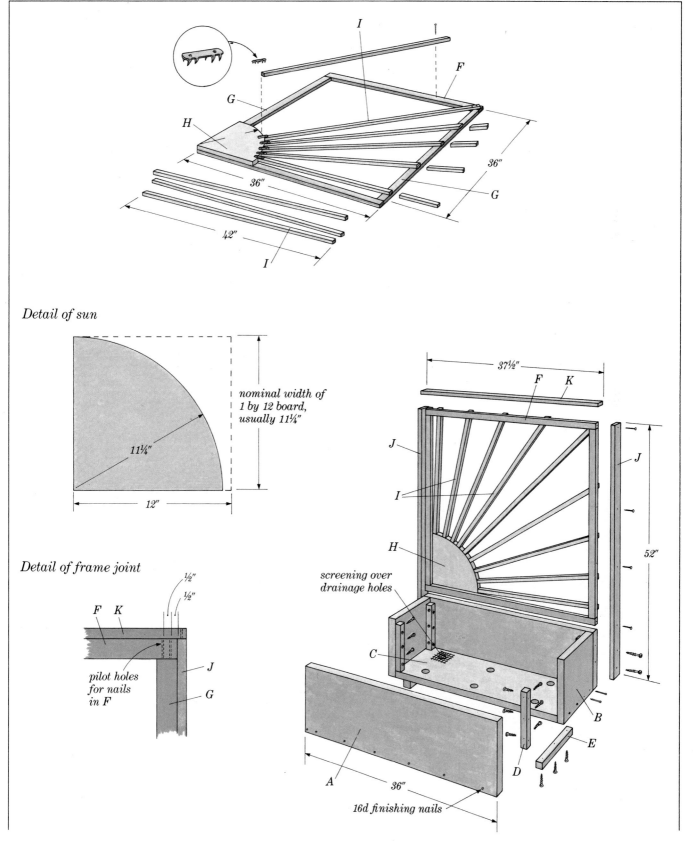

Detail of sun

nominal width of
1 by 12 board,
usually 11¼″

11¼″

12″

Detail of frame joint

½″
½″

F K

pilot holes
for nails
in F

J

G

36″

36″

36″

42″

I

I

G

F

37½″

F K

J

J

I

H

52″

screening over
drainage holes

C

A

36″

16d finishing nails

B

E

D

H

These projects will help make working in the garden a pleasurable experience. Storing and transporting garden accessories, cleaning up, and potting will be easier using the task-oriented projects included here.

This attractive Hose Box protects the hose from the sun, and conceals cumbersome lengths that might be a hazard if left on the ground.

The box in the photograph is made of 2-inch lumber, but because 1-inch stock is adequate and less expensive, that's what we've called for in the instructions.

1. Cut front and back (A), ends (C), top slats (G), and compartment partition (F). Cut feet (E), top braces (H), and front trim (B).

2. Use 6-penny (6d) galvanized box nails to attach sides to back. Measure and cut base (D) to fit, and drill a couple of ¾-inch drainage holes in it. Then nail it in place through sides and back with 6d nails. Turn box over and install feet flush with sides. Use 6d nails through feet into sides, ends, and base.

3. Install front trim flush with top of box front with 3d galvanized box nails. Next, attach front to base of box with two 2-inch brass butt hinges. Position hinges as shown in the illustration, and make small pilot holes for screws with an awl or push drill.

4. Lay top slats (G) on a flat surface with 1-inch spacing between them. Nail top braces (H) to slats with 3d galvanized box nails, centering braces so they clear box front, back, and sides. Install two 2-inch brass butt hinges at back of top, first making pilot holes for mounting screws. Next, place top in position on box and mark location of hinge screws on back of box. Remove top, make pilot holes for screws, then install screws and hinges.

5. Install hooks on ends of front, and position eyes on sides. After deciding where box will be placed, drill a 1½-inch hole for hose in side of box that will be closest to faucet.

6. Miter ends of compartment partition (F) at a 45-degree angle. Glue and nail partition in place with waterproof glue and 3d nails.

Materials List

1x10 surfaced redwood
2 pieces 35" long for (A) front and back
2 pieces 23" long for (C) ends

1x6 surfaced redwood
4 pieces 35" long for (G) top slats
1 piece 17" long for (F) compartment partition

1x4 surfaced redwood
4 pieces 3" long for (E) feet
4 pieces 21" long for (H) top braces

1x2 surfaced redwood
1 piece 35" long for (B) front trim

¾" exterior-grade plywood
1 piece 23"x33½" for (D) base

Hardware and miscellaneous
3d galvanized box nails
6d galvanized box nails
4 brass butt hinges 2", with screws
2 hook and eye sets 1½"
Waterproof glue

This attractive Hose Box provides an alternative to hanging a garden-hose wheel on the wall of your house.

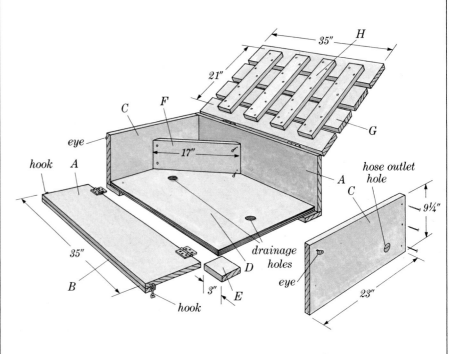

Placed around a garden faucet, this Spigot Surround provides clean footing and a platform where you can coil a hose or prepare a garden spray mixture.

1. Cut long slats (A) and short slats (B). Cut spacers (C) from redwood lath, or rip ¼-inch-thick strips from 2 by 4 stock.

2. Glue a spacer at each end of a long slat with waterproof glue. Coat other side of spacers with glue, and nail another slat through spacers into first slat with 8-penny (8d) galvanized box nails. As you proceed, continue to check that top and bottom surfaces remain flat and ends square.

3. After you glue and nail 5 long slats together, continue with short slats. Place a spacer at each end of all short slats, and glue and nail them in place. Then install remaining spacers and long slats.

4. Measure ends and inside dimensions of assembled board, and cut end trim (D) and inside trim (E) to fit. Using six 8d nails per side, glue and nail end trim pieces to ends of slats. Glue and nail inside trim to exposed ends of short slats inside the square opening.

Materials List

2x4 surfaced redwood
10 pieces 21¼" long for (A) long slats
8 pieces 5½" long for (B) short slats
2 pieces cut to fit for (D) end trim
2 pieces cut to fit for (E) inside trim

¼"x1½" or ⁵⁄₁₆"x1½" redwood lath
36 pieces 3½" long for (C) spacers

Hardware and miscellaneous
8d galvanized box nails
Waterproof glue

Simple Duckboard

You can easily make a simple duckboard for use in wet or muddy areas by nailing 2 by 4 slats to 2 by 4 or 2 by 3 rails placed on edge. Cut notches in rails so that slats are flush with tops of rails, or—for a quick version—simply nail slats directly to tops of rails. See page 11 for information on how to cut notches.

Assemble the duckboard on a flat surface, using 8d galvanized box nails and waterproof glue. Since this project may be wet much of the time, it is a good idea to coat it thoroughly with a wood sealer or preservative.

Simple Duckboard

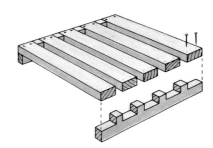

Top. *Easy-to-make duckboards are useful in many parts of the garden.* **Above.** *The Spigot Surround helps keep your garden neat and feet dry.*

Spigot Surround

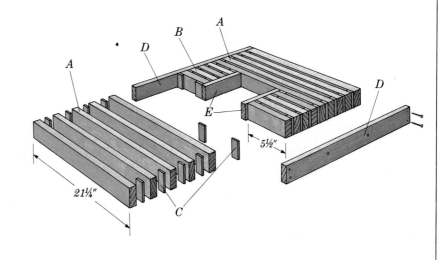

Tote Box

After a day in the garden with this handy Tote Box, you'll wonder what you did without it. It's ideal for carrying sprays, dusts, and tools, which can be hooked onto the pegboard panel. You can remove the panel and use the box to tote nursery transplants, or fill it with an arrangement of plants to display them.

1. Cut sides (A), ends (B), uprights (E), dividers (D), cleats (F), partition (G), and handle (H).

2. Glue and screw sides to ends with waterproof glue and No. 8 flat-head wood screws. Then measure and cut base (C) to fit, and glue and nail it in place with 6-penny (6d) galvanized box nails through sides and ends.

3. Drill a ¾-inch hole in center of each upright, 1 inch from top, for handle. Saw corners off top of uprights. Next, center an upright on one side of each divider and attach with 4 No. 8 screws through divider. Attach cleats to insides of uprights with waterproof glue and 3d galvanized finishing nails. Position cleats flush with bottom of uprights and centered horizontally, allowing a ¼-inch groove between them. Check that partition slides easily in groove.

4. To ensure that partition will fit between uprights, glue and screw one upright assembly in place 4 inches from end of box, as shown in the illustration. Then place partition in its slot and install the other upright against end of partition.

5. Slip dowel handle into place and drill a ⅛-inch hole through each upright and into handle. Secure handle

with 2 No. 8 screws. Remove screws and slip handle out when you want to remove partition.

Materials List

1x6 surfaced redwood
2 pieces 24″ long for (A) sides
2 pieces 10½″ long for (B) ends
2 pieces 18″ long for (E) uprights
2 pieces 10½″ long for (D) dividers

Parting stop ½″x¾″
4 pieces 14″ long for (F) cleats

½″ exterior-grade plywood
1 piece 10½″x22½″ for (C) base

¼″ pegboard
1 piece 11½″x14″ for (G) partition

Hardwood dowel ¾″ dia
1 piece 18″ long for (H) handle

Hardware and miscellaneous
3d galvanized finishing nails
6d galvanized box nails
34 flat-head wood screws 1¼″x#8
Waterproof glue

The Tote Box is sure to have many uses in the garden, from transporting plants and equipment to storing tools. It even makes an attractive plant display.

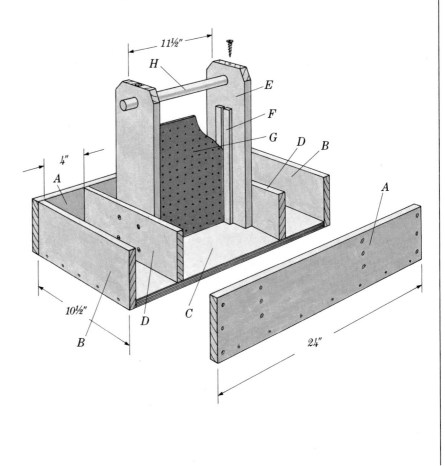

Tote Bench

This portable Tote Bench is another indispensable item for the gardener. Stand on it for extra reach—first making sure that it rests firmly on level ground—or sit on it to do chores more comfortably.

1. Cut legs (B) to length. Lay out the rounded V cut on one leg and remove wood with a coping or power saber saw. Trace cut onto second board, and cut out.

2. Rip-cut rail stock to 4½ inches in width, then cut rails (C) to length. Cut top (A), hinge support (G), front trim (E), and side trim (F). Use a lighter or darker contrasting piece of wood to make trim, if desired.

A handy, portable Tote Bench is useful for sit-down garden jobs. You can carry the tools you'll need in the bench's enclosed storage compartment.

3. Lay out and cut the ¾-inch-deep by 4½-inch-long notches for rails on front and back edges of legs. Glue and nail rails into notches with waterproof glue and 6-penny (6d) galvanized box nails.

4. Next, cut base (D) to size and nail it in place with 6d nails through sides and rails. Attach hinge support to back rail with glue and 3d galvanized finishing nails.

5. An easy way to make handle slot in top is to drill a 1½-inch hole on centerline of top, 4¾-inches from one side. Use a large-diameter bit or a hole saw on a power drill. Drill another hole the same distance from the other side. Then use a saber or coping saw to cut a slot between holes. Sand rough edges.

6. Glue and nail side and front trim to top with 3d nails. Then, using an awl or push drill, make small pilot holes in back edge of top for hinge screws, and install the 2-inch brass butt hinges. Place top in position, and mark hinge screw locations on hinge support. Make pilot holes for screws, and mount hinges.

7. Screw in a hook and eye or a hasp, centered in the front, to latch lid to box. Base can be additionally reinforced by gluing and nailing extra pieces of ¾-inch trim stock into the corners between base and legs.

8. Finish the Tote Bench by sanding all surfaces smooth.

Materials List

2x12 surfaced redwood
2 pieces 11¼" long for (B) legs

1x6 surfaced redwood
2 pieces 14½" long for (C) rails

1x12 surfaced redwood
1 piece 14½" long for (A) top
1 piece 13" long for (D) base

1x2 surfaced redwood
1 piece 14½" long for (G) hinge support

¾"x¾" redwood trim
1 piece 16" long for (E) front trim
2 pieces 11¼" long for (F) side trim

Hardware and miscellaneous
3d galvanized finishing nails
6d galvanized box nails
2 brass butt hinges 2" with screws
1 hook and eye set or hasp with screws
Waterproof glue
80–120-grit abrasive paper as needed

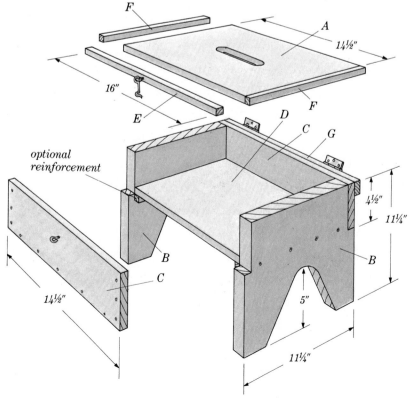

optional reinforcement

Basic Sawhorses

Sawhorses are useful and versatile gardening aids. Two styles are featured here: a Hinged Sawhorse that folds and stores easily, and a Garden Working Horse with a shelf.

Garden Working Horse

This sawhorse is very sturdy and easy to make. If you don't need the shelf, leave it out; the sawhorse will be lighter and just as strong.

1. Cut rail (A), legs (B), braces (C), and stretchers (D). With a power saw, cut a 20-degree bevel along both sides of rail so legs will lie flat against rail. Cut a matching 20-degree miter on both ends of each leg, making sure cuts are parallel. Lay the four 2 by 4s side by side with ends lined up, and cut all legs at once.

2. To attach legs to rail, drill 2 small pilot holes through each leg, side by side and ¾ inch from top of leg. Drill holes at a 20-degree angle parallel with top of leg and top of rail. Next, place legs against rail and use holes as guides to drill ³⁄₁₆-inch pilot holes in rails. Attach legs with No. 10 flat-head wood screws.

3. Lay sawhorse on its side and install the first stretcher 9 inches up from bottom of legs, flush with outside edges of legs. Make small pilot holes through stretchers into legs with an awl or push drill, and install two 1½-inch by No. 8 screws at each end. Flip sawhorse over and repeat for the other stretcher.

4. Place sawhorse on a level surface and screw braces in place with No. 8 screws, making sure that both pairs of legs are spread to the same width at the bottom. Make small pilot holes for screws. After braces are attached, trim their ends flush with legs.

5. Turn sawhorse over, measure distances between stretchers and braces, and cut shelf (E) to fit. Nail it in place through bottom edges of braces and stretchers with 8-penny (8d) galvanized box nails.

Materials List

2x6 surfaced redwood
1 piece 30" long for (A) rail

2x4 surfaced redwood
4 pieces 26" long for (B) legs

1x4 surfaced redwood
2 pieces 22" long for (C) braces
2 pieces 24" long for (D) stretchers

¾" exterior-grade plywood
1 piece 14½"x24" for (E) shelf

Hardware and miscellaneous
8d galvanized box nails
8 flat-head wood screws 2"x#10
16 flat-head wood screws 1½"x#8

Hinged Sawhorse

This folding sawhorse is called a Tennessee Walker. The legs hang straight down for easy storage when you pick up the horse.

1. Cut rail (A) and legs (B). Cut a 20-degree miter on both ends of each leg. (Cuts on each end are parallel.) Place the four 2 by 4s side by side and make the angle cuts across all of them at once.

2. Screw 1 butt hinge to the end of each leg so hinge pin is centered over acute (pointiest) angle and hinge is centered on width of leg. Then screw legs to bottom of rail so edges of outside legs are 3 inches from ends of rail. Position inside legs next to outside legs. Hinge pins should be centered over opposite edges of the rail (see detail illustration). When legs are folded they should just slide past each other.

Materials List

2x4 surfaced redwood
1 piece 36" long for (A) rail
4 pieces 29" long for (B) legs

Hardware and miscellaneous
4 brass butt hinges 3", with screws

These two simple sawhorses can be used not only as construction aids, but also as supports for a plant display, workbench, and dining table.

Garden Working Horse

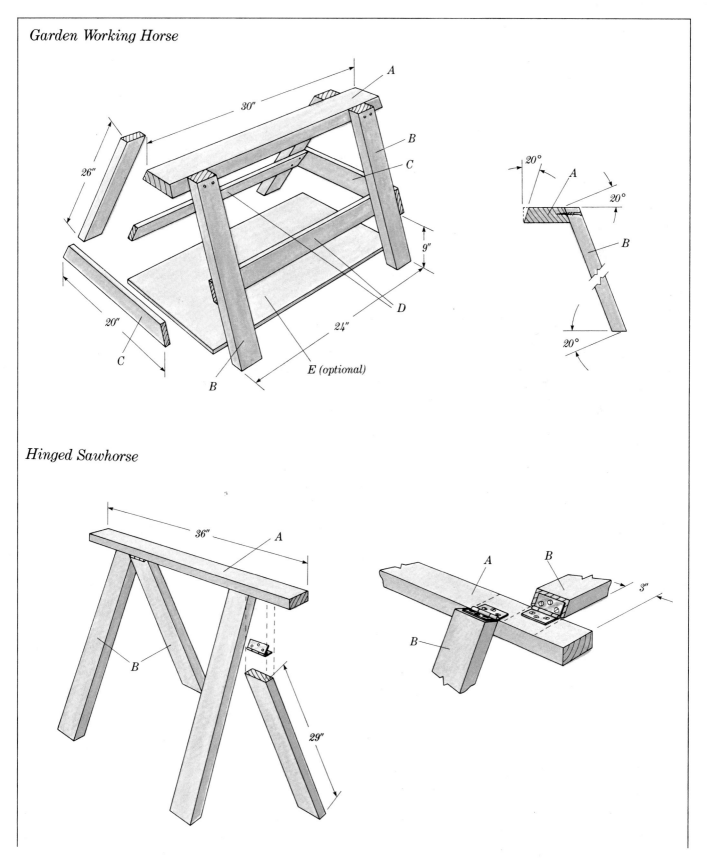

30"

26"

20"

24"

9"

A

B

C

D

C

B

E (optional)

20°

20°

20°

A

B

Hinged Sawhorse

36"

29"

3"

A

B

A

B

B

Roll-Around Sawhorse

Not an ordinary sawhorse, this is really a work platform with plenty of enclosed storage. It will be right at home in your garden and can do double duty next to the barbecue.

It is easy to make and is strong enough to house most of your gardening tools. You can make it with wheels or leave them off if portability is unimportant.

To give this sawhorse a more finished, decorative appearance,

⅝-inch textured plywood made for house siding was used. It comes in many styles; check your building-supply outlet for a style and color you like. You can also use regular ⅝-inch exterior-grade plywood if you prefer.

1. Begin construction by cutting sides (A), ends (B), top (I), legs (F), braces (G), and end trim (D). Cut front and back trim (E) from ¾-inch-square trim stock, or rip from 1-by stock.

This combination sawhorse, storage box, and work platform is great for storing barbecue accessories, garden equipment, outdoor toys, woodworking tools, and much more. The addition of wheels makes it especially practical in the garden.

2. Assemble box first. Use waterproof glue and 8-penny (8d) galvanized box nails to attach ends to sides. Then cut base (C) to fit, put it in place, and glue and nail it to sides and ends with 8d nails.

3. To allow legs to fit snugly against box and extend outward for stability, top of each leg must be beveled. Carefully cut through edge of one leg at a 15-degree angle, then use it as a pattern to make the other legs. Next, cut a 75-degree miter on the other (bottom) end of each leg. Smooth sharp edges of leg ends with abrasive paper.

4. Drill two ⅜-inch holes for leg-mounting bolts through top ends of legs. Make holes perpendicular to side of box, centered and aligned vertically. Place legs on sides of box 4 inches in from ends and transfer leg bolt holes to box sides by tracing through leg holes with a pencil. Drill ⅜-inch holes through marks, then attach legs to box sides with ⅜-inch carriage bolts, washers, and nuts. Use 2-inch bolts in upper holes and 2½-inch bolts in lower holes.

5. After legs are secure, attach braces to legs with waterproof glue and 2 No. 8 screws per leg. Position brace approximately 6 inches from bottom of leg, and make sure both sets of legs are spread to exactly the same width. Make pilot holes with an awl or push drill, then install screws. Cut off ends of braces flush with outside edges of legs. Cut shelf (H) to fit, then place it on top of braces and nail it in place with 8d nails.

6. Edges of top are framed with trim pieces. Use waterproof glue and 6d galvanized finishing nails to attach 1 by 2 end trim to top. Then attach ¾-inch front and back trim with 4d galvanized finishing nails.

7. Screw the 2-inch butt hinges to back of top, then place top in position on box and use hinges as templates to mark screw locations on outside of box. Make small pilot holes with a push drill, and screw hinges in place. If desired, attach a hasp to front of lid and box to hold box closed.

8. Purchase wheels before selecting steel rod stock for axles, so that axle diameter will match diameter of holes in wheels. Attach axles to bottom of legs with pipe straps and sheet-metal screws. Place a couple of washers over the axle, then slide wheels on. Wheels can be held in place with ready-made axle caps hammered onto ends of axle. You can also drill holes in ends of axles and use cotter pins to hold wheels in place.

Materials List

⅝″ exterior siding veneer plywood
2 pieces 7¼″x36″ for (A) sides
2 pieces 7¼″x10¾″ for (B) ends
1 piece 10½″x33″ for (I) top
1 piece 10¾″x34¾″ for (C) base
1 piece approximately 14″x30″ for (H) shelf (cut to fit after braces are in place)

2x4 surfaced redwood
4 pieces 23″ long for (F) legs

1x4 surfaced redwood
2 pieces 24″ long for (G) braces

1x2 surfaced redwood
2 pieces 10½″ long for (D) end trim

¾″x¾″ redwood trim
2 pieces 36″ long for (E) front and back trim

Hardware and miscellaneous
8d galvanized box nails
6d galvanized finishing nails
4d galvanized finishing nails
4 carriage bolts ⅜″x2″, nuts, washers
4 carriage bolts ⅜″x2½″, nuts, washers
8 flat-head wood screws 1½″x#8
Hasp (optional)
8 pan-head sheet-metal screws 1¼″x#6
2 steel rods ⅜″x28″
8 galvanized washers ⅜″
4 wheels 5″, with ⅜″ hubs and axle caps
4 pipe straps ½″
2 brass butt hinges 2″, screws
Waterproof glue
80–120-grit abrasive paper as needed

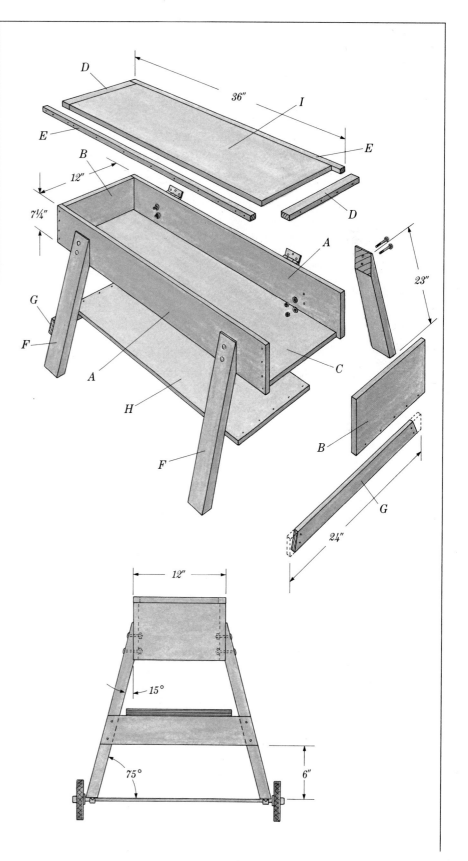

Potting Tables

These easy-to-construct tables can be used for watering, feeding, dividing and repotting plants, or for mixing soil. Instructions for both a crossed-leg and a straight-leg version are given here.

Crossed-Leg Potting Table

1. Begin construction of the crossed-leg version by cutting top boards (A) and top cleats (B). Place top cleats on a flat surface and apply waterproof glue. Position top boards on top cleats so that cleats are straight and 3 inches from ends of tops. Then nail tops and cleats together with 8-penny (8d) galvanized box nails.

2. Choose a table height that will be most comfortable for you. A height in the 30-inch to 36-inch range will probably work best (30 inches if you plan to sit while working; 36 inches for standing). Cut legs (C) to 48 inches (you'll cut them again later). Stack 2 legs with ends aligned and tack them together temporarily with a nail in the exact center. Open them

to an X configuration, with outside edges of legs spread to exactly the width of the tabletop at the height you have selected for your table (minus thickness of tabletop).

3. Using a framing square, draw cut lines for miter cuts at tops and bottoms of legs. Make lines square with a vertical centerline. Unfasten boards and make cuts, then use these pieces to mark the other 2 legs. When all leg boards are cut, flip tabletop over and install an inside leg first by making a pilot hole with a push drill, and gluing and screwing leg to top cleat with waterproof glue and two 2-inch by No. 14 wood screws. Next install outer leg by gluing and screwing it to top. Make pilot holes and install screws through tabletop into leg.

4. To install lag screws in legs, drill two $3/16$-inch pilot holes lined up vertically in center of legs where they cross. Install lag screws and washers.

5. Make sure legs are perpendicular to top, then hold a brace (D) in position (an assistant may be helpful) and mark cut lines on brace. Hold scrap

The Crossed-Leg Potting Table (above) and its straight-leg counterpart can be used for tending plants or as buffets next to the barbecue.

Crossed-Leg Potting Table

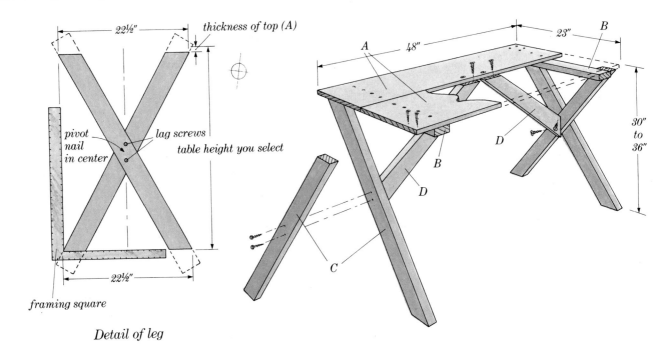

Detail of leg

blocks of 2 by 4 against brace ends parallel to legs and parallel to tabletop, as shown in the illustration. Draw cut lines on brace along edges of scrap pieces. Make cuts, and then attach brace by gluing and screwing it in place, centered on joint in tabletop, with two 2-inch by No. 14 wood screws at each end. Make pilot holes for the screws.

6. Repeat this procedure for mounting the other set of legs. You may have to adjust the final bevel of bottoms of legs so table doesn't rock. Sand all surfaces smooth.

Materials List

1x12 surfaced redwood
2 pieces 48″ long for (A) top

2x4 surfaced redwood
2 pieces 22½″ long for (B) top cleats
4 pieces 48″ long for (C) legs
2 pieces 33″ long for (D) braces

Hardware and miscellaneous
8d galvanized box nails
4 lag screws ¼″x2½″, washers
16 flat-head wood screws 2″x#14
Waterproof glue
80–120-grit abrasive paper as needed

Straight-Leg Potting Table

1. Begin construction of straight-leg table by cutting legs (C), top cleats (B), braces (D), top (A), and shelf (E).

2. Since this table has straight legs, it is easier to assemble legs, cleats, and braces first, then add top and shelf.

Use 8-penny (8d) galvanized box nails and waterproof glue to attach top cleats to legs. Note that cleats are positioned flat, with narrow sides against legs. Attach braces to legs at any convenient height with glue and 8d nails. Make sure both braces are the same distance from bottom of legs so shelf will be level.

3. Glue and nail top pieces to leg assemblies, keeping legs flush with

ends of top. Use 8d nails. Glue and nail shelf pieces in place.

4. Before glue dries, set completed table on a flat, level surface. Check that joints are square, and make sure that all legs are in contact with ground. If any of the legs fail to touch, place heavy objects on table until glue dries. When glue is completely dry, sand all surfaces smooth.

Materials List

2x4 surfaced redwood
4 pieces 36″ long for (C) legs
2 pieces 22½″ long for (B) top cleats
2 pieces 22½″ long for (D) braces

1x12 surfaced redwood
2 pieces 48″ long for (A) top
2 pieces 45″ long for (E) shelf

Hardware and miscellaneous
8d galvanized box nails
Waterproof glue
80–120-grit abrasive paper

Straight-Leg Potting Table

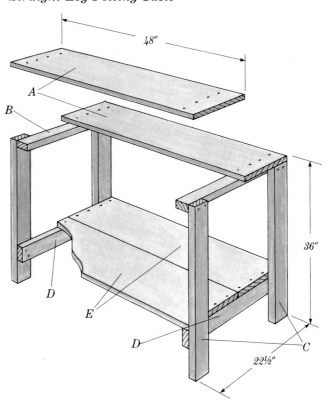

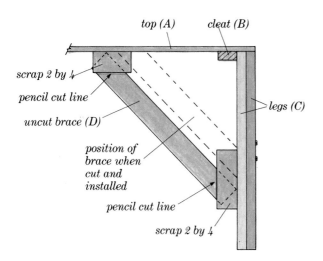

Detail of brace for crossed-leg table

Vegetable Cleanup Table

Here's a special table you can use to top vegetables and remove soil before bringing them into the kitchen. This is also a handy project for anglers who need a place to clean their catch. Ours includes a cutout for a bar sink, but a plastic wash basin will work as well. Simple plumbing allows you to connect a garden hose for running water.

1. Begin construction by cutting top (A), shelf (G), rails (B), cross rails (C), shelf supports (F), and legs (D).

2. Assemble table frame first by nailing rails to the 2 end cross rails with 16-penny (16d) galvanized box nails.

3. Next, attach legs. Place a leg in each corner of frame, flush with top of frame. Drill 3/16-inch pilot holes through rails and cross rails into legs, then drill 3/4-inch-diameter by 3/8-inch-deep counterbores into rails for dowel plugs. Drill 3 holes into each leg—2 from one side, 1 from the other—and stagger them so screws don't meet. Using a socket wrench, attach legs with 1/4-inch lag screws and washers.

4. Cut stretchers (E) to fit exactly between legs, then nail them to shelf supports with 16d nails. Nail this assembly to legs, driving nails through shelf supports into legs. We placed shelf 6 inches from bottom of legs, but it can be installed at any convenient height. Just make sure stretchers are level.

5. Tighten lag screws into legs, and glue plugs into counterbores with waterproof glue. When glue is dry, sand plug ends flush.

6. Notch 2 outer shelf boards to fit around legs, then space shelf pieces evenly on supports, and glue and nail them in place with 8d galvanized box nails. Next, place top pieces on table so that they overhang equally on both ends and on both sides. Glue and nail them in place with 16d galvanized finishing nails.

7. Plumbing for the cleanup table can be as simple as a plastic pail. If

you decide to install a sink, follow manufacturer's directions for cutting rough opening. After opening is cut, install remaining 2 cross rails by nailing them to rails and to underside of top pieces outside sink cutout.

8. Make the water supply from 3/4-inch-diameter PVC water pipe. Attach pipe to end of tabletop and shelf with 3/4-inch galvanized pipe straps. (You'll need to attach a 3-inch-thick filler block to end of shelf and affix pipe to that, as shown in the illustration.) Connect end of pipe to garden hose with a plastic hose adapter attachment.

9. Sink drain can be made from either 1 1/2-inch-diameter plastic pipe or car radiator hose. Lead pipe or hose to one of the legs and secure it with 1 1/2-inch pipe straps. Run hose to ground, and lead it several feet from table to where water can soak into ground without making area around table muddy.

Top. *This handy table provides both running water and an elevated work space right in the garden. Use it for cleaning vegetables or for flower arranging.*
Above. *A plastic tub is the simplest sink to install.*

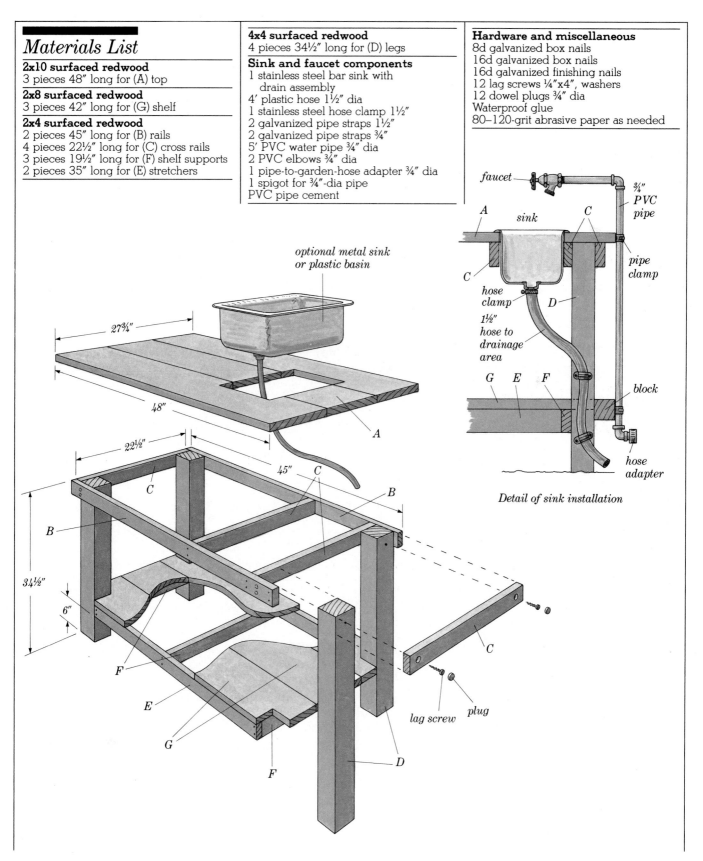

Materials List

2x10 surfaced redwood
3 pieces 48″ long for (A) top

2x8 surfaced redwood
3 pieces 42″ long for (G) shelf

2x4 surfaced redwood
2 pieces 45″ long for (B) rails
4 pieces 22½″ long for (C) cross rails
3 pieces 19½″ long for (F) shelf supports
2 pieces 35″ long for (E) stretchers

4x4 surfaced redwood
4 pieces 34½″ long for (D) legs

Sink and faucet components
1 stainless steel bar sink with
    drain assembly
4′ plastic hose 1½″ dia
1 stainless steel hose clamp 1½″
2 galvanized pipe straps 1½″
2 galvanized pipe straps ¾″
5′ PVC water pipe ¾″ dia
2 PVC elbows ¾″ dia
1 pipe-to-garden-hose adapter ¾″ dia
1 spigot for ¾″-dia pipe
PVC pipe cement

Hardware and miscellaneous
8d galvanized box nails
16d galvanized box nails
16d galvanized finishing nails
12 lag screws ¼″x4″, washers
12 dowel plugs ¾″ dia
Waterproof glue
80–120-grit abrasive paper as needed

faucet

¾″ PVC pipe

A

sink

C

C

pipe clamp

hose clamp

D

1½″ hose to drainage area

G *E* *F*

block

hose adapter

Detail of sink installation

optional metal sink or plastic basin

27¾″

48″

A

22½″

45″ *C*

C

B

B

34½″

6″

F

E

G

F

D

C

lag screw *plug*

Compost Bin

Most gardens produce bushels of refuse. Any nonwoody plant cuttings such as grass clippings, leaves, and tops from a vegetable or flower garden can be composted to yield an excellent mulch and soil conditioner.

This Compost Bin holds generous amounts of refuse, and is designed to provide the air circulation necessary for proper decomposition.

1. Begin construction by cutting footings (A), posts (B), dividers (D), back rails (G), and covers (E). Cut filler strips (F) and divider supports (C).

2. Assemble the two ends first. Nail posts (B) to divider supports (C) so that sides of divider supports are flush with outside edges of posts. Use 16-penny (16d) galvanized box nails and nail from the 2 by 6 post. Then nail one post assembly flush with front end of footing (A), and the other set back 1 inch from the back end of footing, nailing from footing up into post with 16d nails.

3. Install dividers (D) on both ends of bin. Attach top and bottom dividers first, then nail center divider in place. Use 10d galvanized box nails through dividers. Note that all dividers are nailed flush with post at back of partition and are set back 1 inch from edge of front post to allow room for door boards (H).

4. Nail filler strips (F) to divider supports between dividers at front of partitions. Use 8d nails. Strips fill in spaces between dividers and form a continuous slot for door boards.

5. Assemble the 2 center partitions in the same way, but nail divider supports to centers of posts. Then nail 3 dividers to each side of supports and attach filler strips. Nail covers (E) to lower inside dividers to close off pocket formed by these dividers and footings. Use 10d nails.

6. Place the 4 partitions on level ground in the location where you plan to place compost bin. Give footings several liberal coats of an approved preservative, allowing it to dry between coats.

7. Nail back rails (G) to the 2 end partitions first with 8d nails. Check position of partitions; they should be square with back rails. Move bin into its final location, leveling ground first if necessary.

Making your own mulch from kitchen and garden refuse can benefit your garden and your budget.

8. Drive the 2 outer galvanized pipe supports into ground with a sledge-hammer. Keep them tight against faces of end posts, and secure them to posts with pipe straps and galvanized sheet-metal screws. Make sure partition posts remain plumb.

9. Position the 2 center partitions 3 feet in from each end, and attach them to rails with 16d nails. Check that partitions are square with rails and that posts are plumb, then pound in remaining pipe supports and attach pipe clamps with sheet-metal screws. Measure distances between divider supports in each section and cut door boards (H) to fit in slots.

10. If you plan to stain or coat bin with preservative, do it before applying wire cloth. Then nail cloth to dividers and back rails with galvanized staples.

Materials List

2x6 rough redwood
4 pieces 60″ long for (A) footings
8 pieces 34½″ long for (B) posts

1x6 rough redwood
18 pieces 54″ long for (D) dividers
3 pieces 108″ long for (G) back rails
10 pieces cut to fit for (H) door boards

1x1 redwood trim
12 pieces 8″ long for (F) filler strips

1x4 rough redwood
2 pieces 48¼″ long for (E) covers

2x4 rough redwood
8 pieces 34½″ long for
   (C) divider supports

Galvanized water pipe ¾″
4 pieces 6′ long

Hardware and miscellaneous
16d galvanized box nails
8d galvanized box nails
10d galvanized box nails
12 galvanized pipe straps ¾″
24 galvanized sheet-metal screws
   1″x#8
45′ galvanized wire cloth (½″ mesh),
   36″ width
Galvanized staples
Wood preservative

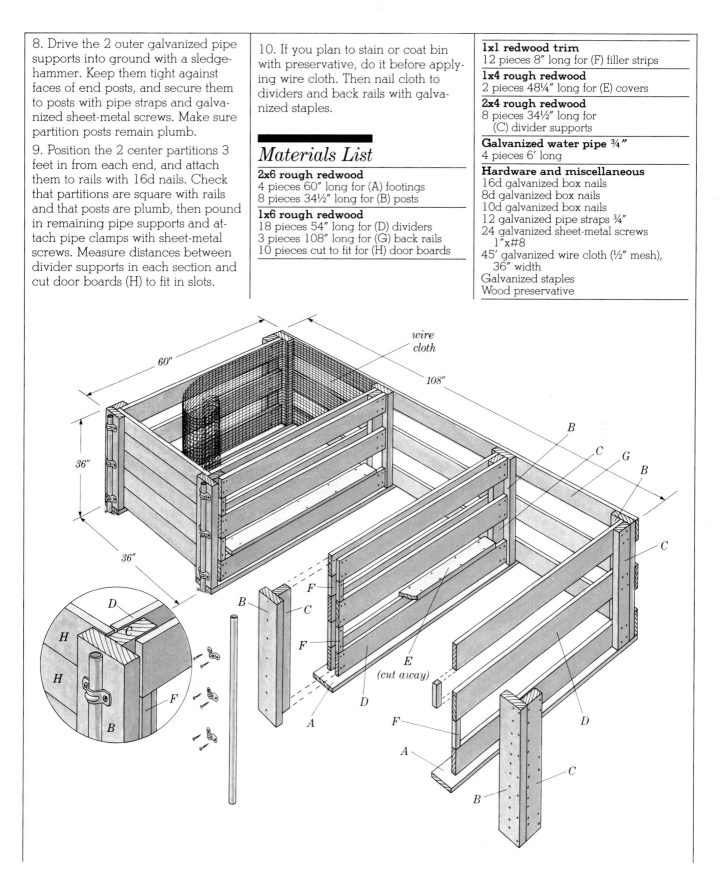

OUTDOOR FURNITURE
Duckboard Tables and Benches

The outdoor furniture in this section allows you to expand your living and playing space by bringing your family outdoors. All these projects are designed for carefree living and casual entertaining.

Whether building the simple projects for the beginner or the more challenging pieces that require additional tools and skill, the results are functional pieces of furniture that you and your family can put to use in your garden.

This versatile table is nothing more than a section of duckboard. The other duckboard projects in this book are designed to be used around wet and muddy areas. Yet, just as a duckboard makes a sturdy platform to stand on, it can also be used as a tabletop, bench, or display platform—all you have to do is add legs.

1. Begin construction by cutting spacers (A) and slats (B). Cut leg assembly of your choice; all designs are cut from 2 by 4 stock.

2. Follow directions under step 2 of the Deck-Top Bench (page 71) for determining which side of slats will face up, and mark boards.

3. Glue and nail 3 spacers to ends and center of 1 slat with waterproof glue and 3-penny (3d) galvanized box nails. Place nails toward edges of spacers to allow room for dowel holes. Repeat this procedure for each slat, carefully centering middle spacer on each one.

4. Stack slats on their sides on a flat surface, aligning ends carefully. Lay out and drill ½-inch-diameter dowel holes through slats in centers of spacers. Clamp slats together temporarily to keep them in position while drilling. Use a doweling jig to align a power drill, or carefully drill freehand with a spade bit. When you reach

depth of the drill bit, unstack slats and use the last complete hole as a guide to continue drilling through next group of slats.

5. When all holes are drilled, insert dowels, apply glue to dowels and mating surfaces of slats and spacers, and clamp. When glue dries, chip off excess with a sharp chisel, cut off extra dowel, and sand top smooth.

6. For short legs, glue and nail short feet (E) and short rails (F) together with 8d nails. For tall legs, use ¼-inch by 3-inch lag screws and glue to join tall feet (C) and rails (D). Drill ³⁄₁₆-inch pilot holes for screws. If desired, drill counterbores so you can conceal screw heads with dowel plugs. Then insert screws with a socket wrench and glue plugs into holes. Attach short legs or tall legs to bottom of duckboard top with waterproof glue and ¼-inch by 2½-inch lag screws and washers. Drill ³⁄₁₆-inch pilot holes for screws.

7. If you choose to make the H-legs, lay out and cut a ¾-inch-deep notch in sides of duckboard to form a half-lap joint for upper part of legs. Cut a 3½-inch-wide by ¾-inch-deep notch

on inside of legs (G) to form the other half of this joint. Attach legs to rails (H) with glue and ¼-inch by 3-inch lag screws, then simply set top on legs. As in tall leg design, screw heads can be concealed with dowel plugs glued into counterbores.

Materials List

¼″x3½″ finished redwood bender board
33 pieces 8″ long for (A) spacers

2x4 surfaced redwood
12 pieces 60″ long for (B) slats
4 pieces 9″ long for (C) tall feet
4 pieces 17″ long for (D) tall rails
    or 4 pieces 3″ long for (E) short feet
2 pieces 18″ long for (F) short rails
    or 4 pieces 16″ long for (G) H-legs
4 pieces 17¾″ long for (H) H-rails

Hardwood dowel, ½″dia
3 pieces 24″ long

Hardware and miscellaneous
3d galvanized box nails
8d galvanized box nails (for short legs)
4 lag screws ¼″x2½″, washers (for tall legs or short legs)
16 lag screws ¼″x3″, washers (for tall legs or H-legs)
16 dowel plugs ¾″–1″ dia (optional for tall legs or H-legs)
Waterproof glue
80–120-grit abrasive paper

Sections of duckboard—simple to construct—make attractive and practical plant displays and benches.

Since duckboard construction is so basic, these projects are easy and quick to modify for a variety of uses. The leg designs shown can be adapted to any top, and most can be lengthened to any reasonable height. The ones illustrated differ slightly from those in the photographs to give you an idea of the many variations possible.

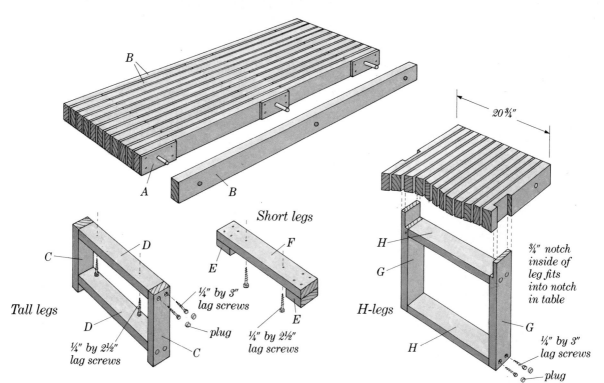

B

A

B

20 ¾"

Tall legs

C

D

D

C

¼" by 2½" lag screws

¼" by 3" lag screws

plug

Short legs

E

F

E

¼" by 2½" lag screws

H-legs

H

G

G

H

¾" notch inside of leg fits into notch in table

G

¼" by 3" lag screws

plug

X-Base Bench

The classic X-Base Bench and the H-Base variation on the opposite page are easy to construct and suitable for the garden. Use them for seating or for displaying plants. Quantities in the Materials List make one bench.

1. Cut tops (A), legs (B), rails (C), and filler blocks (D).

2. Assemble legs first. Use 8-penny (8d) galvanized finishing nails and waterproof glue to attach filler blocks to the centers of 2 legs. Tack each set of legs together temporarily with a nail through exact center. Spread legs to 12½-inch width at top and bottom outside edges, and glue and nail to sides of rails with 8d nails. Use top edge of each rail as a guide to cut angle at top of legs, then cut a parallel angle at bottom of each leg.

3. Drill a ³⁄₁₆-inch pilot hole through filler block and both legs for the lag screw. Insert lag screw and tighten. Repeat this procedure for assembling the other set of legs.

4. Another method of constructing a set of X-legs is to cut a notch ¾ inch deep by 2½ inches wide through both opposing leg pieces and join legs where they cross with a half-lap joint. Both legs can then be glued and nailed to the same side of the rail.

5. Attach tops to leg assemblies with waterproof glue and 16d galvanized finishing nails. Countersink nail heads with a nail set, and fill holes with wood putty.

Materials List

2x8 surfaced redwood
2 pieces 60" long for (A) tops

2x3 surfaced redwood
4 pieces 22" long for (B) legs
2 pieces 12½" long for (C) rails
2 pieces 2½" long for (D) filler blocks

Hardware and miscellaneous
8d galvanized finishing nails
16d galvanized finishing nails
2 lag screws ¼"x4"
Waterproof glue
Wood putty

This X-Base Bench was constructed with spacers between the legs, but for extra strength and a more finished look it can also be made with a half-lap joint where legs cross.

|← 11" →|

|← 14½" →|

|← 18½" →|

Bench width options

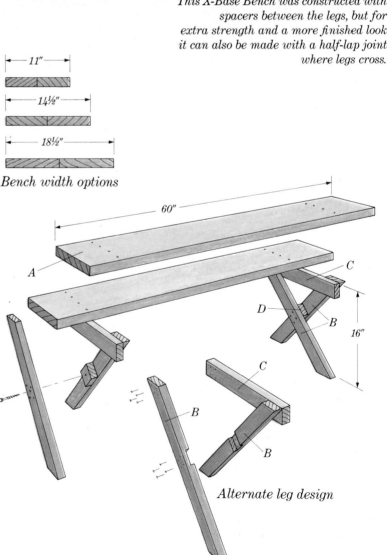

Alternate leg design

S everal different leg designs for this simple bench are illustrated below. If you decide to design your own, remember that considerable rocking and twisting forces are at work on the legs, so always glue and nail, or glue and screw, all joints together. Quantities in the Materials List make one bench.

1. Begin construction by cutting tops (A), legs (B), braces (C), and rails (D).

2. Assemble legs first. Place legs and braces in position on a flat surface. Locate braces halfway up legs. Mark dowel locations on legs and braces at the same time with a try square or carpenter's combination square.

3. Use a doweling jig to drill the 1¼-inch-deep by ½-inch-diameter dowel holes. Apply glue to joint and to dowel ends, and assemble legs and braces. Check that they are flat, then clamp until glue dries.

If you don't have a doweling jig, cut 2 pieces of 1 by 3 stock to 12½ inches. Glue and nail these pieces to both sides of the brace and to the legs with 8-penny (8d) galvanized finishing nails and waterproof glue.

4. Attach rails to legs with 8d nails. Note that rails are positioned with their edges against legs.

5. Finish bench by gluing and nailing tops to leg assemblies with water-proof glue and 16d nails. Set nails and fill holes with putty.

Materials List

2x8 surfaced redwood
2 pieces 60" long for (A) tops

2x3 surfaced redwood
4 pieces 14" to 17" long for (B) legs
2 pieces 7½" long for (C) braces
2 pieces 12½" long for (D) rails

Hardware and miscellaneous
8d galvanized finishing nails
16d galvanized finishing nails
8 grooved hardwood dowels ½"dia x 2"
Waterproof glue
Wood putty

This variation on the conventional X-Base Bench is also quite simple to make. Leg joints are doweled for strength.

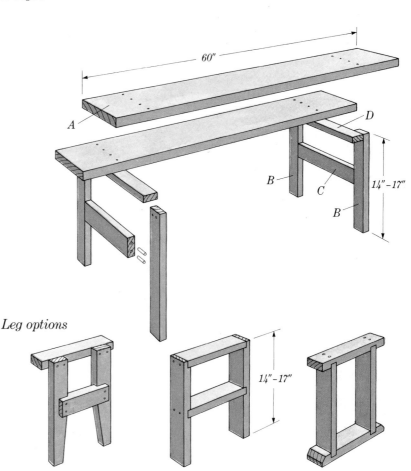

Leg options

Fire-Pit Benches

A set of four Fire-Pit Benches doubles as a table cover that conceals the pit. Two of the benches have legs that run the length of the base; the other two are made with open bases.

These distinctive benches can be used individually or as modules that form a table cover for a fire pit. Separate them to provide campfire seating; stack them to serve as a high table or a bar. Our project includes two open and two closed benches that will span fire pits up to 30 inches in diameter.

1. Begin construction by cutting tops (A), short legs (B), and long legs (C).

2. Carefully lay out and cut 6-inch-deep by 1½-inch-wide notches in short and long legs. Center notches in short legs, and make them approximately 5 inches from ends of long legs. After you cut each notch, check its fit; all parts should slip together without being forced. If you have to force two parts together, eventually they will split.

3. Assemble legs with glue, then attach tops with glue and 16-penny (16d) galvanized finishing nails. Make pilot holes for nails, then drive 4 nails through top into each leg section. Drive 2 or 3 additional nails through top into central section of long legs. Countersink nail heads with a nail set. If desired, fill holes with dark, mahogany-colored putty. Sand all surfaces thoroughly.

Materials List

2x12 surfaced redwood
4 pieces 52½" long for (A) tops
12 pieces 11¼" long for (B) short legs
2 pieces 52½" long for (C) long legs

Hardware and miscellaneous
16d galvanized finishing nails
Waterproof glue
Wood putty (optional)
80–120-grit abrasive paper

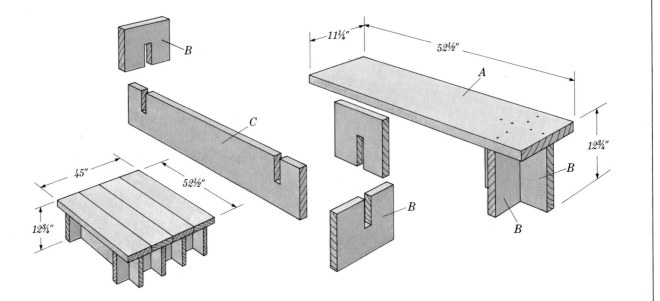

Deck-Top Bench

The attractive slat design of the Deck-Top Bench promotes quick drainage of rainwater and facilitates cleaning.

nail. Then drive a nail through slat into each dowel to lock it in place.

5. Repeat procedure to install remaining slats. Make ¼-inch-thick spacers from scrap wood. To maintain even spacing, temporarily put spacers between slats as you glue and nail them together. Drive all nails into bottom of bench. After installing last slat cut each dowel flush.

6. Position and temporarily nail or clamp rails onto legs, making sure they are perpendicular and that legs are inset 2 inches from ends of rails. Use 10d nails. Lay out and drill ³/₁₆-inch pilot holes through rails and into legs for the ¼-inch by 4-inch lag screws. Put screws on opposite diagonals from each side, so they will clear each other.

7. Assemble legs and rails with glue and lag screws, checking that legs remain square. You may first want to drill ³/₈-inch-deep by ⅝-inch-diameter counterbores for lag-screw heads. Attach leg assemblies to bottom of bench with ¼-inch by 6-inch lag screws. Using an extra long ³/₁₆-inch bit, drill pilot holes through rails. Insert lag screws in rails so their tips protrude, and use tips to mark screw locations on slats. Drill pilot holes in slats, then put legs in place and tighten screws.

8. Sand surface of bench thoroughly.

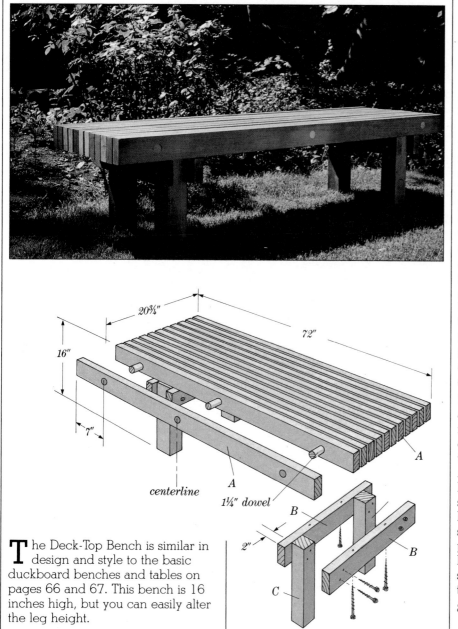

centerline

1¼" dowel

A

B

B

C

2"

The Deck-Top Bench is similar in design and style to the basic duckboard benches and tables on pages 66 and 67. This bench is 16 inches high, but you can easily alter the leg height.

1. Cut slats (A), rails (B), and legs (C). Use standard 3-foot lengths of 1¼-inch-diameter closet pole for dowels (D).

2. Sight down length of each 2 by 4 slat from one end, holding a narrow dimension up. Many of the boards may be slightly warped or crowned in this plane. Mark side of each piece with an arrow so that convex edge will become top surface of bench.

3. Lay out locations of dowel holes on one slat. Mark a hole 7 inches in from each end of slat and a third hole in center of slat. Drill 1¼-inch-diameter holes with a spade bit, then use this slat as a template to drill other slats.

4. Assemble bench top by applying waterproof glue to dowel ends, then inserting a dowel into each hole in the first slat. Align dowel ends flush with slat side. Drill a ⅛-inch pilot hole through bottom of slat into dowel for a 10-penny (10d) galvanized box

Materials List

2x4 surfaced redwood
12 pieces 72" long for (A) slats
4 pieces 20¾" long for (B) rails

4x4 surfaced redwood
4 pieces 12½" long for (C) legs

Hardwood dowel 1¼"dia
3 pieces 24" long for (D) dowels

Hardware and miscellaneous
10d galvanized box nails
16 lag screws ¼"x4", washers
8 lag screws ¼"x6", washers
Waterproof glue

Table Bases

T ables are centers for many out-door activities. Their structures should be uncomplicated, strong, and durable. Here are two designs for table bases; the first supports a 36-inch-round or -square top, the second a 36-inch by 48-inch rectangular top.

The designs are simple enough so you can modify them to suit your exact needs. If you decide to make larger tables, increase length or width by at least 24 inches for each additional seat. Remember that table height must permit comfortable seating, so adjust the height if you have unusually high or low chairs.

Square Base

1. Cut rails (A) and legs (B).

2. Rails fit together with a simple half-lap joint. Make notches by pairing up rails, clamping them together, and marking their centers. Then lay out and cut a 1½-inch-wide by 1¼-inch-deep notch in center of each rail. You can use a radial-arm or table saw with a dado attachment. To cut notches by hand, make a saw cut at each edge of notch and several in between, then remove wood with a sharp chisel. Test fit of rails in notches. Notches must be

This simple design makes for a strong table base that will support either of the tabletops on the following pages. Tables will seat four to six comfortably, depending on the size of the top.

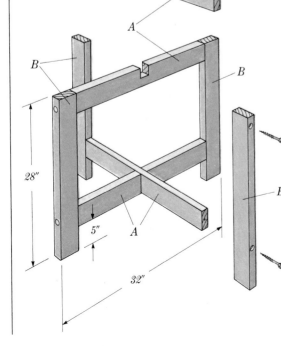

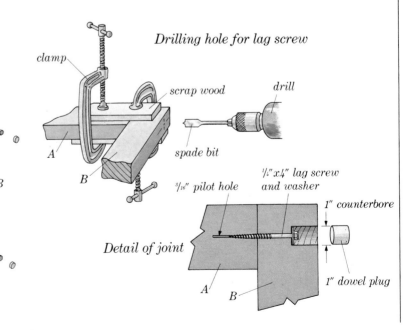

72

deep enough so that edges of rails are flush with each other.

3. Clamp together 2 opposing legs to top and bottom rails with scrap wood, as shown in the illustration. Place rails so notches are facing up, and position top rail flush with top of leg, bottom rail 5 inches up from bottom of leg. Drill 3-inch-deep by $^3/_{16}$-inch-diameter pilot holes for lag screws through both legs into centers of rails, $1^1/_4$ inches from top and $6^1/_4$ inches from bottom of legs. Then, using these holes as guides, drill $^7/_8$-inch- or 1-inch-diameter counterbores to accommodate washers and dowel plugs. Install lag screws with a socket wrench, but do not tighten them all the way.

4. Assemble other half of base in the same way, but with rail notches facing down. Once holes are drilled, remove bottom rail, put second half of base in place over first half, and then put lower rail back in place. Apply glue to notches and fit both sections together with rails seated in their notches. Adjust fit and clamp

joints until glue sets. Then apply glue to rail ends and tighten lag screws.

5. Cut dowels to fit and glue into counterbores. Set base on a flat, level surface with weighted boards across rails until glue dries. Sand all surfaces lightly, sanding dowel ends flush.

Materials List

2x3 finished redwood
4 pieces 27" long for (A) rails
4 pieces 28" long for (B) legs

$^7/_8$" or 1" dia dowel
8 pieces cut to fit

Hardware and miscellaneous
8 lag screws $^1/_4$"x4", washers
Waterproof glue
80–120-grit abrasive paper as needed

Rectangular Base

1. Cut legs (A), rails (B), top supports (C), braces (D), and stretcher (E). Taper legs, as shown in the illustration, if desired.

2. Use waterproof glue and 16-penny (16d) galvanized box nails to attach legs to braces, then to top supports.

3. Apply glue to sides of legs and ends of top supports where rails will make contact. Position each rail, then nail it to ends of top supports. Drill $^1/_4$-inch holes through ends of rails and tops of legs. Insert carriage bolts and washers, and tighten nuts.

4. Glue and nail stretcher in place. Apply glue to both ends, and drive 16d nails through leg supports into ends of stretcher.

5. Set table base on a flat, level surface, and place weighted boards across top until glue dries. Sand the base smooth.

Materials List

2x4 surfaced redwood
4 pieces 29" long for (A) legs
2 pieces 42" long for (B) rails
2 pieces 29" long for (C) top supports
2 pieces 26" long for (D) braces
1 piece 38" long for (E) stretcher

Hardware and miscellaneous
16d galvanized box nails
4 carriage bolts $^1/_4$"x3$^1/_2$", nuts, washers
Waterproof glue
80–120-grit abrasive paper as needed

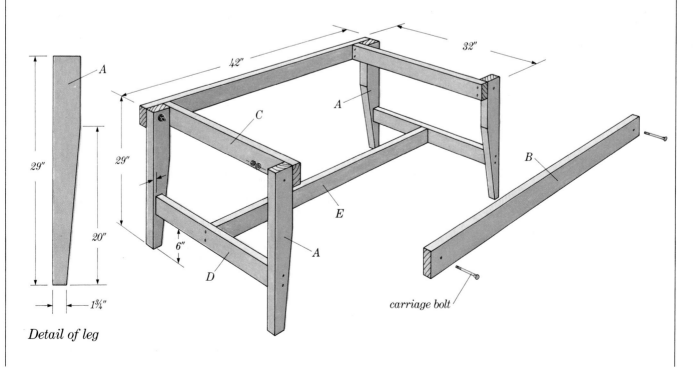

Detail of leg

carriage bolt

Round Tabletop

The top for an outdoor table can be made from a variety of materials. A piece of solid wood or plywood can be used, or plywood can form the base for another material such as hardwood, vinyl floor tiles, ceramic tiles, or plastic laminates. Some of these possibilities are illustrated on page 75.

This Round Tabletop is made from lengths of 1 by 6 lumber.

1. Cut all top boards (A), (B), and (C), and edges (D). If you want tabletop to be smooth, without grooves, plane edges of top boards square. (Tabletop in photograph is made of pine, which is sanded square at the mill and thus does not require edge planing to make a smooth surface.)

2. Lay out top boards as shown and match them for best fit and grain, then number each board.

3. Pair up boards and place them side by side. Use a carpenter's combination square to mark locations of dowels on edges of both boards at the same time, then follow these marks to position a doweling jig. Place dowels on 6-inch centers. Drill 1¼-inch-deep by ⅜-inch-diameter holes for dowels.

4. Apply glue to dowels and all mating surfaces, insert dowels, and clamp boards together. Place tabletop on a flat, level surface while glue sets. After glue dries, turn table over and nail edge pieces in place. Use glue and a few 3-penny (3d) galvanized box nails at ends and middle, as shown. If you plan to use the square base from the previous page, allow at least 33 inches from corner to corner to accommodate legs.

5. Scribe on the top a circle with a radius of 18 inches, and cut to shape with a saber saw. Use a small-toothed finish blade, and tape along cut line with masking tape to avoid splintering edges. Once table is cut, secure edge pieces with additional 3d nails.

6. Carefully sand tabletop and edges with a sanding block and abrasive paper. If you have a router, you may want to chamfer table edges or use a decorative edge cutting bit.

7. For a removable tabletop, secure top to base with plated angle braces screwed to legs and underside of top. For a permanent attachment, use flat-head wood screws. Drill pilot holes and counterbores through tabletop into rails, install screws, and glue dowel plugs into counterbores.

Materials List

1x6 surfaced redwood
3 pieces 37" long for (A) long tops
2 pieces 33" long for (B) medium tops
2 pieces 27" long for (C) short tops
4 pieces 27" long for (D) edges

Hardware and miscellaneous
3d galvanized box nails
32 grooved hardwood dowels ⅜"x2"
Waterproof glue
Masking tape as needed
Sanding block
80–120-grit abrasive paper
4 plated angle braces, screws (optional)
4 flat-head wood screws 1¾"x#12 (optional)
4 dowel plugs, ⅞" or 1" dia, for top (optional)

This handsome tabletop is joined with dowels for strength and durability. The one in the photograph is made of pine, but redwood will last longer outdoors.

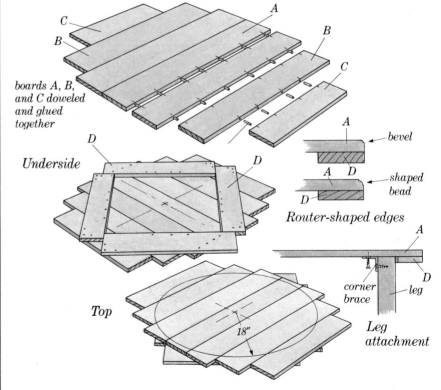

boards A, B, and C doweled and glued together

Underside

Top

18"

bevel

shaped bead

Router-shaped edges

corner brace

leg

Leg attachment

Like the Round Tabletop on the opposite page, the Rectangular Tabletop is joined with dowels for strength. This top is the easier of the two to construct.

1. Begin construction of rectangular top by cutting top pieces (A). Since the corners of finished redwood stock are rounded at the mill, the tabletop will have grooves in it unless you plane edges of all boards square, as was done for the Rectangular Tabletop in the photograph.

2. Using dowels will strengthen joints in tabletop. See directions for round top (steps 2–4 on page 75), and follow them to lay out holes and install dowels, but use ½-inch dowels in this heavier stock. Then glue top boards together and clamp them until glue sets, making sure ends stay square and top stays flat. After glue sets, remove excess with a sharp chisel.

3. Measure and cut end pieces (B) to exact width of table, and plane edges square if desired. Lay out and mark dowel locations on end pieces and edges of tabletop. Drill dowel holes with a doweling jig, insert dowels, glue ends to tabletop, and clamp. Place tabletop on a flat, level surface while glue sets.

4. After glue dries, sand all surfaces smooth, removing any glue that was squeezed out. Attach top to base with plated corner braces on the underside, or with flat-head wood screws installed down through the top (see step 7, opposite page).

Materials List

2x4 surfaced redwood
11 pieces 41½" long for (A) tops
2 pieces approximately 38½" long for (B) ends

Hardware and miscellaneous
82 grooved hardwood dowels ½"x2"
Waterproof glue
80–120-grit abrasive paper
4 plated angle braces, screws (optional)
4 flat-head wood screws 3½"x#12 (optional)
4 dowel plugs, ⅞" or 1" dia, for top (optional)

This Rectangular Tabletop rests on the Square Base (page 72). The design can easily be altered to make a longer table by adding more cross members and lengthening end pieces.

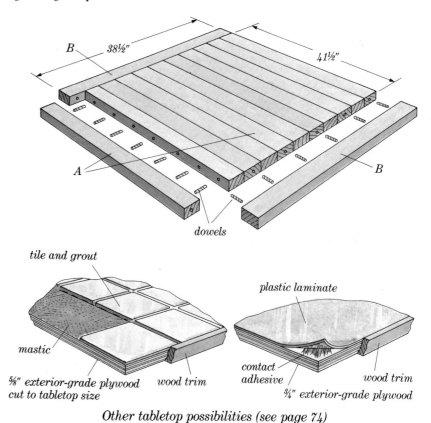

B   38½"   41½"   B

A   dowels

tile and grout   plastic laminate

mastic   wood trim   contact adhesive   wood trim

⅝" exterior-grade plywood cut to tabletop size   ¾" exterior-grade plywood

Other tabletop possibilities (see page 74)

Umbrella Table and Chairs

This umbrella table and its matching chairs are two projects designed to bring you and your family together outdoors. These projects are more challenging than most because they require joinery skills and a table or radial-arm saw.

Umbrella Table

1. Begin construction of the table by cutting legs (A) to rough length. Cut top supports (B), the 3 lengths of top pieces (C), (D), and (E), and bottom supports (F).

2. Lay out top pieces, matching them for best fit and grain pattern. Then number them and mark the joint edges so you will be able to match boards after you drill dowel holes.

3. Use a carpenter's combination square or try square to mark dowel locations on mating edges at the same time. Space dowels 6 inches apart. Then use these marks to position doweling jig. Drill 1¼-inch-deep by ⅜-inch-diameter holes for dowels.

4. After all holes are drilled, apply glue to edges of 2 long top pieces. Then apply glue to dowel ends and push them into holes in one side. Place the other board on dowels, put a piece of scrap against opposite edge, and hit scrap with a hammer to drive boards together. Glue up remaining boards, then clamp top assembly together. Check that top is flat before you set it aside to dry.

5. Clamp top supports (B) and bottom supports (F) together and cut the ¾-inch-deep by 5½-inch-wide leg dadoes in each set at the same time. Cut a 1¾-inch-deep by 3½-inch-wide dado to form the half-lap joint in center of bottom supports. Then cut a ¾-inch-deep by 3½-inch-wide dado in center of top supports.

6. Temporarily assemble top and bottom supports. Mark ends of these boards so you will round the correct edge. Then separate boards and use a coping or band saw to cut curves on each end of bottom and top supports. Glue each set of supports together with waterproof glue, and nail from the bottoms, using 3-penny (3d) galvanized box nails for top supports and 8d or 10d galvanized box nails for bottom supports. Keep nails away from center of joint where umbrella stem will go.

7. Stack top supports centered on bottom supports and clamp together. Drill a small-diameter pilot hole all the way through boards, and use an electric drill with a hole-saw attachment to bore a 1½-inch hole (check diameter of umbrella stem) through top supports and partially through bottom supports.

8. Enlarge leg pattern on cardboard and cut it out to form a template. Place template on rough-cut leg pieces and trace around it. Cut legs to shape with a coping or saber saw, or stack them and cut with a band saw. Draw a line across leg pieces 3¾ inches from bottom and 1½ inches from top. Round over leg edges with a router or abrasive paper, except above and below these marks (this area is in dado joint and should be left square).

9. Assemble table base by gluing legs to both sides of one of the bottom supports. Check that legs are plumb, and clamp until glue dries. Then glue and clamp top supports to legs. Next, glue remaining legs to the other

This Umbrella Table with its set of chairs provides a shady place to relax in the garden.

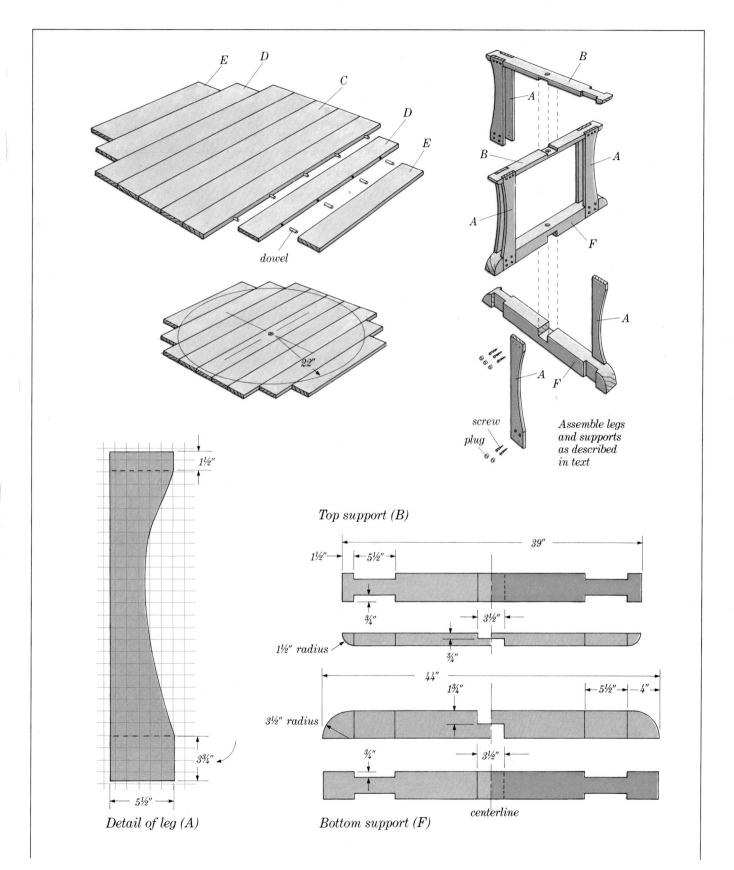

E   D   C   D   E

dowel

22"

B   A

B   A

A   F

A

A   F

screw
plug

Assemble legs
and supports
as described
in text

1½"

3¾"

5½"

Detail of leg (A)

Top support (B)

39"

1½"   5½"

¾"

3½"

1½" radius   ¾"

44"

1¾"

5½"   4"

3½" radius

¾"   3½"

centerline

Bottom support (F)

bottom support and top support. Check alignment of pieces, and place base on a flat, level surface to dry.

10. When glue dries, install screws at tops and bottoms of legs. Lay out and drill small pilot holes for screws with ⅜-inch counterbores for plugs. Use a combination counterbore bit to drill both holes at the same time, or use separate bits, drilling pilot holes first. Install the 1¾-inch by No. 8 flat-head wood screws, and glue plugs into counterbores.

11. Finish tabletop by cutting it into a circle. Drive a small nail into the center and use a nonstretchable string to guide a pencil as you draw a 22-inch-diameter circle. Tape along cut line with masking tape to avoid splintering edges, then use a coping, saber, or band saw to cut table round. Chip away any excess glue with a sharp chisel, then sand all surfaces smooth. Round top edge with a router, or use a vibrating sander or a sanding block.

12. Attach tabletop to base by making small pilot holes up through top support into bottom of table, then installing four 2½-inch by No. 8 flat-head wood screws per support.

Materials List

1x6 surfaced redwood
8 pieces 27½" long for (A) legs

2x4 surfaced redwood
2 pieces 39" long for (B) top supports

2x6 surfaced redwood
5 pieces 45" long for (C) long tops
2 pieces 37" long for (D) medium tops
2 pieces 25" long for (E) short tops

4x4 surfaced redwood
2 pieces 44" long for (F) bottom supports

Hardware and miscellaneous
3d galvanized box nails
8d or 10d galvanized box nails
56 flat-head wood screws 1¾"x#8
8 flat-head wood screws 2½"x#8
42 grooved hardwood dowels ⅜" dia x 2"
32 wood plugs ⅜" dia
Waterproof glue
String as needed
Masking tape
Sanding block
80–120-grit abrasive paper

Umbrella-Table Chairs

These chairs are designed to match the umbrella table on the previous pages. Even if you don't build the table, the chairs will be at home on your patio. Use oak or mahogany, instead of redwood, for kitchen or dining-room chairs. Quantities on the Materials List are for four chairs. The seat height of this design is 17 inches; you can adjust the plan accordingly for higher or lower seats.

1. Begin construction by cutting narrow slats (D), wide slats (C), and stretchers (B) to length. Note that narrow slats (D) and stretchers (B) must be additionally ripped to 3-inch widths. Cut top rails (A), lower rails (E), front legs (F), and back legs (G) to length. Rip top rails (A), lower rails (E), and front legs (F) to 3-inch widths.

2. Lay out shape of back legs on the rough-cut 2 by 8 pieces, and cut them to final shape. Note that back slopes at a 10-degree angle from vertical. Round tops with a coping saw or saber saw.

3. Clamp together 2 back legs and 2 front legs to form sets, then lay out and cut the 1-inch-deep by 3-inch-wide rail dadoes in both sets at the same time (2 cuts in back legs, 1 cut in front leg). Then cut the ¾-inch-deep by 3-inch-wide stretcher dadoes in back edges of legs.

4. Cut dadoes for slats (C) and (D) in upper parts of back legs. Make these dadoes ⅝ inch deep. Note that top dado is for wide slat and is 3½ inches wide; the other 2 are 3 inches wide.

5. Clamp top rails (A) together. Then, starting at forward end, lay out and cut slat dadoes. Make them ⅝ inch deep by 3 inches wide, and space them ½ inch apart. Turn rails over and at forward end cut a ¾-inch-deep by 3-inch-wide dado for legs.

6. If you wish to add a decorative detail to chairs, enlarge scroll and heart patterns and transfer them to cardboard. Trace scroll patterns on top and bottom rails, stretchers, and lower back slat. Check illustration to be sure you are cutting decoration in the correct edges. Cut decorative hearts centered in wide slats that will be installed at tops of chairs.

7. On a flat surface, assemble a back leg, front leg, and top and bottom rails with waterproof glue. Use bar or pipe clamps to pull rails tight into leg

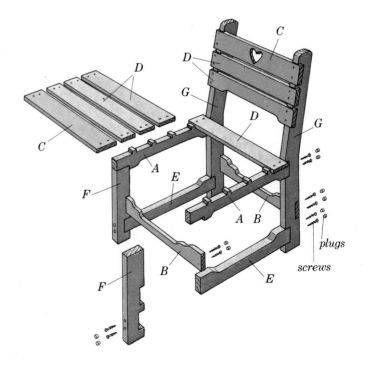

plugs

screws

dadoes, placing clamps on outside of chair. After both sides are glued and clamped, place waxed paper between the flat chair halves and clamp both halves together with C-clamps to insure a flat, true side.

8. When glued leg assemblies are dry, glue, then clamp stretchers to legs. When glue dries, drill small-diameter pilot holes and ⅜-inch counterbores in legs and stretchers for No. 8 screws. (You can use a combination counterbore bit to do this in one operation.) Drill through front and back legs into lower rails, through stretchers into front and back legs, and through back legs into top rails. Then install screws and glue plugs into counterbores. Use 2-inch screws through stretchers and 3½-inch screws through legs.

9. Remove excess glue with a sharp chisel. Sand all edges smooth with a sanding block and abrasive paper. Round upper edges of all slats.

10. Install a wide slat (C) at front of chair first. Note that it is wider than dado and hangs over ½ inch. Use glue and 6-penny (6d) galvanized finishing nails. Then proceed with the narrow slats. Center slats so that there is an even ⅜-inch overhang on each side of rail.

11. Install wide slats with decorative heart cutout at tops of chair backs, and then rest of back slats. Use 6d nails. With a nail set, countersink nail heads ⅛ inch, then apply wood putty to holes. A dark mahogany shade of putty matches new redwood very closely in color.

12. Sand all surfaces thoroughly.

Materials List

1x4 surfaced redwood
24 pieces 19¾" long for (D) narrow slats
8 pieces 19¾" long for (C) wide slats
8 pieces 19" long for (B) stretchers

2x4 surfaced redwood
8 pieces 18" long for (A) top rails
8 pieces 16" long for (E) lower rails
8 pieces 14¾" long for (F) front legs

2x8 surfaced redwood
8 pieces 35" long for (G) back legs

Hardware and miscellaneous
6d galvanized finishing nails
48 flat-head wood screws 3½"x#8
32 flat-head wood screws 2"x#8
80 wood plugs ⅜" dia (can be cut from hardwood dowel or from redwood scrap with a plug bit)
Waterproof glue
Wood putty
Waxed paper
80–120-grit abrasive paper
Sanding block

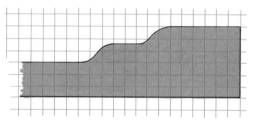

Pattern for stretchers (B) on ½" squares

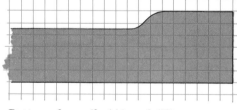

Pattern for rails (A) and (E) and back slat (D) on ½" squares

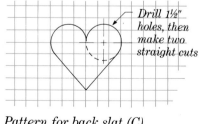

Drill 1½" holes, then make two straight cuts

Pattern for back slat (C) on ½" squares

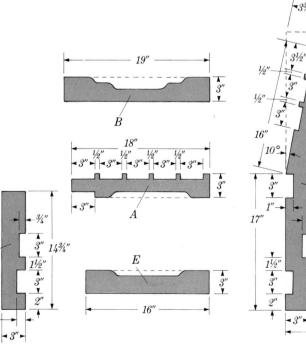

Picnic Table and Benches

The simple lines and classic style of this country picnic table and matching benches make them a handsome addition to any patio or deck. This project is more complicated than some of the others, but the results are worth the extra effort.

Picnic Table

1. Cut top braces (A), stretcher (B), tops (C), leg braces (D), legs (E), horizontal leg supports (F), and center table support (G).

2. Lay out and arrange top pieces according to grain pattern and best fit. Number each board, then pair up boards and use a carpenter's combination square or try square to mark dowel locations on both mating edges at the same time. Mark dowel holes on 6-inch centers. Then use these marks to position doweling jig. Drill 1¼-inch-deep by ⅜-inch-diameter holes for each dowel.

3. Assemble top boards one at a time, applying glue to edges of boards and ends of dowels. Then clamp top together, making sure it is flat.

4. Clamp horizontal leg supports (F) together to form 2 sets. Lay out and cut 1¾-inch-deep by 3½-inch-wide dadoes in each set. Separate parts and bevel ends. Note that dadoes face inside of table and that bevels must be cut opposite one another for upper and lower leg supports.

5. Clamp legs (E) together to form sets. Lay out and cut the 1¾-inch-deep by 3½-inch-wide dadoes at ends of legs. Also cut the 1½-inch-deep by 9¼-inch-wide dadoes for leg braces in the center of the other side of leg sets.

6. Check sizes of ends of stretcher, then lay out mortises on leg braces (D), centered horizontally and 2 inches from bottom edge. Drill small holes in corners of mortise rectangles, then use a coping or saber saw to cut between holes. Square corners of mortises with a chisel, and sand edges smooth.

7. Assemble legs, horizontal leg supports, and leg braces with waterproof glue, making sure legs are plumb. After glue dries, drill small-diameter pilot holes for the 2½-inch by No. 8 screws. Drill 4 holes through legs into leg supports at each joint and 3 holes through leg braces into legs. Use pilot holes as guides for drilling ⅜-inch counterbores for plugs, or use a combination counterbore bit to drill both holes at once.

8. Install screws, then glue plugs into holes. After glue dries, cut off plug heads and sand them flush.

9. Cut a decorative scroll on bottom edge of stretcher as shown in the illustration. Install stretcher through mortises in leg braces so that it extends 1½ inches past outside of each leg. Drill small pilot holes with countersinks through bottoms of leg braces into stretcher, then screw in place with one 3½-inch by No. 8 flathead wood screw per brace.

10. Remove excess glue from tabletop with a chisel. Cut a ¼-inch chamfer on top edge and a ¾-inch chamfer on bottom edge with a router, or sand edges with an electric sander or a sanding block.

11. Place top on frame, centering and aligning it carefully. Mark position of upper horizontal leg supports on table bottom. Remove table, and glue and screw top braces (A) to table using these marks as a guide. Drill 4 small pilot holes per support, then install 2-inch by No. 8 screws.

12. Replace table on frame and lay out and drill six ³⁄₁₆-inch pilot holes, 3 per side, through underside of upper horizontal leg supports (F). Mark drill bit for a 6-inch depth to avoid drilling through tabletop. Drill 1-inch-deep counterbores wide enough to accommodate lag washers, and install ¼-inch by 5-inch lag screws. Use 1 washer per screw.

13. Cut 45-degree bevels on ends of center table support (G), and mount it centered on underside of tabletop using three ¼-inch by 5-inch lag screws. Put 2 or 3 washers on each screw before installing so screws do not go all the way through tabletop.

This large, elegantly designed Picnic Table is likely to get a lot of use for outdoor meals and summer gatherings.

Materials List

2x4 surfaced redwood

2 pieces 40" long for (A) top braces
1 piece 73" long for (B) stretcher

2x8 surfaced redwood
6 pieces 96" long for (C) tops

2x10 surfaced redwood
2 pieces 29" long for (D) leg braces

4x4 surfaced redwood
4 pieces 27" long for (E) legs
4 pieces 37" long for (F) horizontal leg
supports
1 piece 40" long for (G) center table
support

Hardware and miscellaneous
44 flat-head wood screws 2½"x#8
2 flat-head wood screws 3½"x#8
8 flat-head wood screws 2"x#8
9 lag screws ¼"x5", 15 washers
80 grooved hardwood dowels ⅜"x2"
44 wood plugs ⅜" dia
Waterproof glue
80–120-grit abrasive paper
Sanding block (optional)

Benches

1. Cut seat braces (A), stretchers (B), foot halves (C), seats (D), and legs (E).

2. Use glue and six 2½-inch by No. 8 screws per brace to attach seat braces to bottom of seats. Then chamfer upper and lower edges of seats and braces to match table.

3. Cut legs to final shape from rough-cut pieces of 2 by 12 stock. The plans are for a 17-inch-high bench, but you can adjust height to suit. Benches are usually 14 inches to 18 inches high.

4. Lay out and cut mortises for stretcher in center of each leg (see step 6 of table instructions). Clamp foot halves together and cut bevels on ends, then cut a ¾-inch-deep by 8¼-inch-long notch in each foot half to fit around legs. Drill 4 pilot holes with ⅜-inch-diameter counterbores in each set of foot halves, then glue and screw foot halves to bottoms of legs with 1¾-inch by No. 8 screws. Glue plugs into counterbores.

5. Cut decorative detail on bottom edge of stretcher, then assemble legs and stretcher. Position stretcher as you did for table, and secure it with two 2½-inch by No. 8 flat-head wood screws at each end. Make small pilot holes for the screws, and install them at an angle as shown.

6. Position seat pieces on legs, then use a combination counterbore bit to drill pilot holes with ⅜-inch counterbores for plugs in seats. Glue and screw seat assembly to legs with

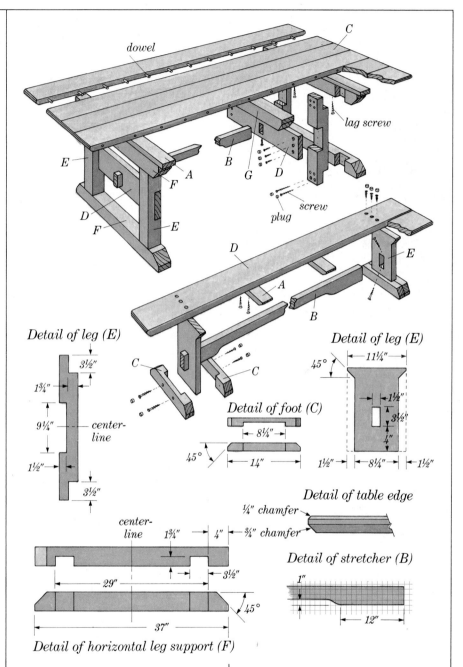

dowel

C

lag screw

E *B* *G* *D* *A* *F*

screw

plug

D *F* *E*

D *A* *E*

B

Detail of leg (E)
3½"
1¾"
9¼" — center-line
1½"
3½"

Detail of leg (E)
45° —11¼"—
—1½"—
3½"
4"
1½" — 8¼" — 1½"

C — *C*

Detail of foot (C)
— 8¼" —
45°
— 14" —

Detail of table edge
¼" chamfer
¾" chamfer

center-line
1¾" 4"
— 29" —
3½"
— 37" —
45°

Detail of stretcher (B)
1"
— 12" —

Detail of horizontal leg support (F)

waterproof glue and 2½-inch screws. Glue plugs into holes. When glue dries cut them flush, and sand all surfaces thoroughly.

Materials List

2x4 surfaced redwood
4 pieces 13" long for (A) seat braces
2 pieces 74" long for (B) stretchers
8 pieces 14" long for (C) foot halves

2x8 surfaced redwood
4 pieces 96" long for (D) seats

2x12 surfaced redwood
4 pieces 15½" long for (E) legs

Hardware and miscellaneous
44 flat-head wood screws 2½"x#8
16 flat-head wood screws 1¾"x#8
40 dowel plugs ⅜" dia
Waterproof glue
80–120-grit abrasive paper

Hibachi Table

Here is another easy-to-make version of a duckboard table. It has a cutout in the center to house a hibachi grill. Check the dimensions of your hibachi and adjust size of hibachi box if necessary. There must be ample room around the hibachi for cooling air to circulate.

Although the hibachi box is insulated with a fireproof material, never leave it unattended while coals are burning, and remove the hibachi from the box after use.

1. Cut hibachi box ends (A) and sides (B), long slats (C) and short slats (D), leg spacers (E), and legs (F).

2. Follow directions under step 2 of the Deck-Top Bench (page 71) for determining which side of slats will face up, and mark boards.

3. Lay out and drill the 1¼-inch-diameter dowel holes in slats, following directions under step 4 of the Basic Duckboard (page 66). Then apply glue to dowel ends (H) and holes in one slat, insert dowels into slat, and

align dowel ends flush with slat side. Make a small pilot hole with an awl or push drill and drive an 8-penny (8d) galvanized box nail through bottom of slat into each dowel.

4. Slip next slat on dowels. Place a ¼-inch-thick piece of lath or scrap between first and second slats to maintain even spacing, then glue and nail second slat in place. After you have joined 5 long slats, install 6 rows of short slats on each end, followed by 5 more rows of long slats. Work on a flat surface, and check to make sure slat edges stay flush so tabletop will be flat and even. When last slat is in place, cut dowels off flush.

Top. The low Hibachi Table is an outdoor grill and dining table in one.
Center. *Well for hibachi must be insulated with a fireproof material. Make air holes in sides and bottom.*
Right. *When you're not cooking, the hibachi cutout can have other uses.*

5. Lay out dowel hole locations on all leg pieces and on bottom of tabletop, checking that leg dowels (N) will penetrate centers of two table slats. Use a spade bit to drill ¾-inch-diameter dowel holes in leg pieces and into bottom of tabletop. Assemble legs and leg spacers with glue and 8d nails. Then glue dowels into legs and underside of table.

6. Nail hibachi box sides to ends with 4d galvanized box nails. Then cut base (G) to fit in box formed by sides and ends, drill holes in it, and nail it in place through sides and ends.

7. Inside of hibachi box can be lined with either ceramic tile, or with a heat-resistant material such as fiberglass cloth. If you use tile, attach tile pieces to inside of hibachi box with mastic, then fill in spaces between tiles with grout. If you use a heat-resistant material, cut aluminum flashing stock to size according to pattern for end trim (L) and side trim (M). Nail flashing in place over lining pieces (I, J, and K) with 2d galvanized box nails. Drill or cut several air holes through material on box bottom.

8. Sand table surface thoroughly.

Materials List

1x6 surfaced redwood
2 pieces 10¾" long for (A) box ends
2 pieces 18½" long for (B) box sides

2x4 surfaced redwood
10 pieces 72" long for (C) long slats
12 pieces 26" long for (D) short slats
2 pieces 21¼" long for (E) leg spacers

4x4 surfaced redwood
4 pieces 21¼" long for (F) legs

¾" exterior-grade plywood
1 piece 9¼"x18½" for (G) box base

Hardwood dowel 1¼" dia
4 pieces 36" long for (H) dowels

Hardwood dowel ¾" dia
4 pieces 9¾" long for (N) leg dowels

⅛"–⅜" heat-resistant material
2 pieces 4½"x8¾" for (I) end liners
2 pieces 4½"x18½" for (J) side liners
1 piece 9"x18" for (K) bottom liner

3"-wide aluminum flashing
2 pieces 11¾" long for (L) end trim
2 pieces 21" long for (M) side trim

Ceramic tile, mastic, grout
as needed (optional for hibachi box lining—use either tile or another heat-resistant material)

Hardware and miscellaneous
2d galvanized box nails
4d galvanized box nails
8d galvanized box nails
Waterproof glue
80–120-grit abrasive paper

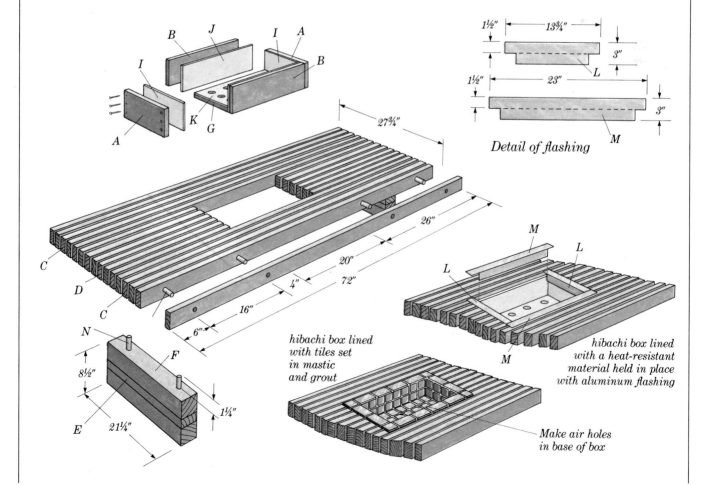

Detail of flashing

hibachi box lined with tiles set in mastic and grout

hibachi box lined with a heat-resistant material held in place with aluminum flashing

Make air holes in base of box

Deck Lounge

This handsome lounge is a welcome addition to patio or deck. The back adjusts from a horizontal to a tilted position that is ideal for reading in comfort. A partially enclosed base creates a storage compartment.

1. Cut side edging (A), back edging (B), back supports (C), end brace (D), back rails (E), and slats (F). Cut back brace (G), foot (H), sides (I), and compartment end (K).

2. Assemble the frame first. Use glue and 16-penny (16d) galvanized box nails to attach sides to end brace and foot. End brace is flush with bottom of sides. Cut compartment bottom (J) to size, then glue and nail it in place with 8d galvanized box nails through sides and end brace. Glue and nail compartment end in place with 8d nails through sides. Drive additional 8d nails through bottom edge of compartment end into base.

3. Starting at the foot, install first slat so it overhangs end of frame by ¾ inch. Use waterproof glue and 4 screws per slat. Drill ⅛-inch pilot holes for the 2¼-inch by No. 8 flathead wood screws, then enlarge upper ¼ inch of each hole to ⅜ inch to accommodate wood plugs. You can use a counterbore drill bit to make both plug hole and pilot hole in one operation. After all screws are tight, glue plugs into holes.

4. Place the 4 backrest slats on a flat surface, and attach back rails to them with waterproof glue and 16d galvanized finishing nails driven through slats. Sink nail heads with a nail set, then fill holes with wood putty.

5. Place backrest assembly face down on fixed platform and align edge of backrest with last fixed slat. Check that backrest is flush with sides of lounge, then install hinges. Cut mortises in edges of slats to recess hinges, if desired. Fold backrest flat and check clearance between sides and back rails.

6. Use glue and 2¼-inch by No. 8 flat-head wood screws to attach back brace to back supports. Then attach this assembly to back rails with ¼-inch carriage bolts. Drill ¼-inch holes for the bolts, centered at top of back supports and in tops of back rails.

7. Glue and screw side and back edging to ends of slats. Drill ⅛-inch pilot holes for screws and ⅜-inch counterbores for plugs. Then insert screws and glue plugs into all holes.

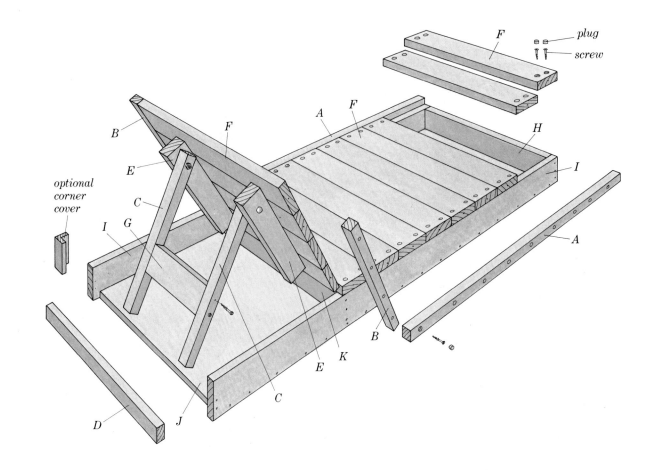

When glue dries, chip away excess with a sharp chisel. Saw heads of wood plugs flush, then sand all surfaces of lounge smooth.

8. You may want to add decorative pieces to hide nail heads at corners of sides, as in photographs. Cut notches in 7¼-inch-long pieces of 2 by 2 stock, as shown in the illustration, and glue them in place.

Materials List

2x2 surfaced redwood
2 pieces 49½" long for (A) side edging
2 pieces 22" long for (B) back edging
2 pieces 24" long for (C) back supports
4 pieces 7¼" long for corner covers (optional)

2x3 surfaced redwood
1 piece 21" long for (D) end brace
2 pieces 20" long for (E) back rails

2x6 surfaced redwood
13 pieces 24" long for (F) slats
1 piece 15" long for (G) back brace

2x8 surfaced redwood
1 piece 21" long for (H) foot
2 pieces 70" long for (I) sides

¾" exterior-grade plywood
1 piece 21"x21" for (J) compartment bottom
1 piece 7¼"x21" for (K) compartment end

Hardware and miscellaneous
8d galvanized box nails
16d galvanized box nails
16d galvanized finishing nails
66 flat-head wood screws 2¼x#8
2 carriage bolts ¼"x3½", nuts, washers
2 brass butt hinges 3", with screws
62 redwood plugs ⅜" dia
Wood putty
Waterproof glue
80–120-grit abrasive paper

Above. *Not all time in the garden should be spent working! Relax on this lounge with adjustable back. The wood blends well with deck and garden surroundings.* **Left.** *Raised backrest reveals storage compartment below.*

Garden Swing

Here's a charming hanging swing sure to provide years of family pleasure. Note that the construction is all done with glue and screws, with half-lap joints at critical points for added strength. All screws are countersunk and plugged for lasting beauty and durability.

1. Begin construction by cutting slats (A), armrests (B), bottom rail (C), and back rail (D). Cut seat supports (E), back supports (F), and armrest supports (G). Note that back supports must be ripped to 4½ inches wide.

2. Begin assembly of frame by first laying out and cutting rabbets on seat supports, back supports, and armrest supports. Lay out ¾-inch-deep by 5-inch-wide rabbet for back supports 17¾ inches from front ends of seat supports. Cut this rabbet in the outside of end seat supports and in one side of middle seat support. Cut it at a 12-degree angle, as shown in the illustration, to give back support a comfortable slant. Note that seat support is longer than necessary and that a corner of back support will extend a little below bottom of seat support. Trim both pieces flush once they are glued together.

This beautifully crafted swing is perfect for lazy days in the shade. It can be hung on a porch as well as from a large tree.

3. Cut ¾-inch-deep by 5½-inch-wide rabbets on bottom ends of back supports, again at a 12-degree angle, to match rabbet in seat support. Cut a ½-inch-deep by 5½-inch wide rabbet in bottom ends of armrest supports.

4. Mark seat contour on one seat support by drawing a shallow arc, about 1 inch deep, from the back support rabbet to a point 6 inches from front of seat support. Remove wood in this area with a saber saw, jigsaw, or band saw. Use this support as a pattern to mark and cut other seat supports. Then cut out small arc on bottom of middle seat support.

5. Apply glue to rabbets in seat supports and back supports, join parts together, and clamp. Glue armrest support rabbets to seat supports and clamp. Position armrest support so back edge lines up with front of arc cut on seat support. When glue dries, remove clamps, make 4 small pilot holes with ⅜-inch counterbores in each joint. Use 1¼-inch by No. 8 screws for back support joint and 2-inch by No. 8 screws for armrest support. Insert screws, then glue dowel plugs into holes.

6. Enlarge armrest pattern, transfer it to rough-cut armrests, and cut them to final shape with a jigsaw or saber saw. Round over all edges with a router or abrasive paper, except where armrests attach to back supports. Attach armrests to top of armrest support and to back support with glue and two 2-inch by No. 8 screws in each joint. Make pilot and ⅜-inch counterbores for screws, and glue dowel plugs into holes.

7. Cut bottom and back rails (C) and (D) to final shape (see detail illustration). Bottom rail must be ripped to 6¼ inches wide before decorative cutout is made. If you want to cut decorative hearts in back rail, enlarge pattern, transfer it to back rail, and cut with a jigsaw or saber saw. You can also design and cut out your own pattern. Round edges of bottom and back rails with abrasive paper.

8. Attach back and bottom rails to side and center assemblies. It is important to keep swing square during this assembly. Working on a flat, level surface or workbench, clamp rails to side assemblies with bar or pipe clamps. Check alignment with a framing square, then drill 2 pilot and counterbore holes through each end of each rail for screws and plugs.

9. Remove bottom rail, apply glue to joint, and reattach rail with 2-inch by No. 8 screws. Remove back rail next, apply glue, and install with 1½-inch by No. 8 screws. Then clamp center assembly in place and repeat drilling, gluing, and screwing procedure. Glue plugs into all counterbores.

10. Sand all slats smooth, and round over top corners with a sanding block, or, if you have a router, use a ⅛-inch roundover bit. Install seat slats, beginning with front and back slats. Place front slat flush with ends of seat supports and glue and screw it into seat supports with 1½-inch by No. 8 screws. Glue and screw back seat slat into seat supports so it is positioned against back supports. Trim ends of second seat slat so it will fit between armrest supports, then glue and screw remaining seat slats in place so they are evenly spaced. There should be about ½-inch spacing between all slats.

11. Install back slats, starting with bottom one by putting it ½ inch from the last seat slat. Then space remaining slats evenly up to back rail. Glue plugs into all screw holes.

When glue dries, cut plugs flush with a sharp chisel and sand everything smooth. Drill two ⅝-inch holes in top of each end back support for back hanging ropes as shown in the illustration. For front ropes, drill one ⅝-inch hole through front of each armrest, one hole through each end of front seat slat, and 2 holes in end of each seat support just in front of armrest support.

12. To hang, thread ½-inch nylon rope through holes at top and at bottom, and tie figure-eight knots to lock it in place.

With 3 or 4 adults in it, the swing is heavy. To hang on a porch, use large hooks threaded deep into ceiling joists of porch. Wall anchors will not hold. If you plan to hang swing outdoors, choose a sturdy tree branch at least 4 or 5 inches in diameter.

Materials List

1x3 surfaced redwood
11 pieces 72" long for (A) slats

1x4 surfaced redwood
2 pieces 26" long for (B) armrests

1x8 surfaced redwood
2 pieces 72" long for (C) bottom rail and
(D) back rail

2x6 surfaced redwood
3 pieces 24" long for (E) seat supports
3 pieces 28" long for (F) back supports

2x4 surfaced redwood
2 pieces 14½" long for (G) armrest
supports

Hardware and miscellaneous
12 flat-head wood screws 1¼"x#8
39 flat-head wood screws 1½"x#8
22 flat-head wood screws 2"x#8
73 dowel plugs ⅜" dia
Waterproof glue
80–120-grit abrasive paper
Sanding block
½" nylon rope, as needed for hanging

Pattern for armrest (B) on 1" squares

¾"-deep dado

to be cut off
after assembly

Pattern for seat support (E)
on 1" squares

cutout on
center support
only

Pattern for curves on rails
(C) and (D) on 1" squares

Drill 2"
holes,
then
make 2
straight
cuts

Heart pattern
on 1" squares

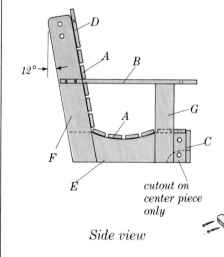

Side view

cutout on
center piece
only

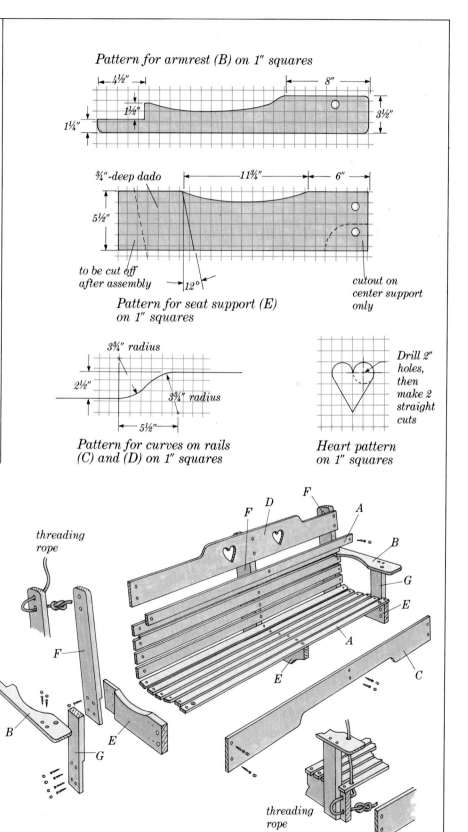

threading
rope

threading
rope

Wading Pool

One look and parents will be as excited as kids about this portable wading pool. The deck keeps pool and kids off the lawn, which otherwise can turn into a sea of mud. The pool itself can be filled with either water or sand.

Be sure to place the finished pool on a soft surface, such as a lawn, since the deck may be slippery when wet. It's also a good idea to put it in a location where you'll be able to keep an eye on the aquatic activities.

1. Cut ends and center brace (A), sides (B), compartment sides (D), decking (I), and compartment bottom pieces (K).

2. Starting at storage compartment end of deck, nail sides to an end with 16-penny (16d) galvanized box nails. Note that end (A) is inset 2 inches from ends of sides. Next, attach compartment bottom pieces to compartment sides with 2-inch by No. 6 multipurpose screws, then attach compartment sides to end with 16d

nails through end, so compartment is centered on end. Nail center brace (A) to other end of compartment sides and to sides with 16d nails.

3. The deck is sized for a pool approximately 42 inches in diameter. Adjust length and placement of supports (C) if your pool is a different size. Cut supports to length, then nail support ends to center brace. Nail remaining end (A) to supports and to sides to complete the basic frame.

4. Cut corner braces (E) to length, then miter both ends at a 45-degree angle. Nail them into corners formed by supports, end, and center brace with 8d galvanized box nails. Then cut and install short and long end supports (M) and (F) in centers of ends to support decking.

5. Cut feet (G) to length, then cut a 45-degree bevel on both ends of feet. Turn frame over and attach feet to bottom of sides, flush with ends, with 16d nails.

6. Install decking next. Starting at pool end, place first board ⅛-inch from end of frame and attach it with 8d nails through decking into sides, braces, and supports. Note that ends of decking are also set back ⅛ inch from outside edges of sides. This creates an attractive shadow line and hides any misalignments that occur.

7. Place a few 16d nails between this board and the next to act as spacers, then nail on second board. Compartment lid is cut from the twelfth, thirteenth, and fourteenth boards. Put these pieces in place, mark cut lines directly over centers of compartment sides, remove boards, and cut them, saving cutout portions. Then reinstall, allowing ⅛-inch clearance along sides of lid. Then attach remaining decking. Rip last piece of decking to fit, leaving ⅛ inch between it and end of frame. Sand smooth all rough corners and edges.

8. To mark pool cutout, drive a nail partway into exact center of pool area. Tie one end of a string around a pencil and the other end around the nail so string is exactly the radius of the pool cutout you need. Then mark circumference of pool on deck. Allow for a snug fit between rim of pool and decking to prevent stubbed toes. Use a saber saw to cut decking.

9. Check overall dimensions of deck frame, then cut end trim (H) and side trim (J) to length. Miter end trim pieces and nail them to end supports and sides. Miter side trim and nail it to sides and end trim, but not to decking. Use 8d nails through trim.

10. Cut cleats (L) to length, then glue and nail cutout portions of deck pieces to them with 8d nails, allowing spaces between planks to match pool decking. Make sure cleats are at least ¾ inch in from ends of deck pieces so they will clear compartment sides (D). For a neater look, cut bottom corners off cleats at a 45-degree angle. Drill the 1-inch finger holes in centers of 2 outside lid pieces.

Kids will enjoy having their own deck and pool on hot summer days. This design includes a built-in storage compartment under the deck.

Materials List

2x6 surfaced redwood
3 pieces 54" long for (A) ends and center brace
2 pieces 86" long for (B) sides
2 pieces 31½" long for (D) compartment sides
1 piece 6" long for (F) long end support
1 piece 2" long for (M) short end support

2x4 surfaced redwood
2 pieces 42" long for (C) supports
4 pieces 18" long for (E) corner braces

1x4 surfaced redwood
2 pieces approximately 60" long for (H) end trim
2 pieces approximately 90" long for (J) side trim

1x6 surfaced redwood
16 pieces 56¾" long for (I) decking
6 pieces 19" long for (K) compartment bottom

2x2 surfaced redwood
4 pieces 18" long for (G) feet
2 pieces 15" long for (L) cleats

Hardware and miscellaneous
16d galvanized box nails
8d galvanized box nails
24 galvanized multipurpose screws 2"x#6
1 plastic wading pool approximately 42" dia
Waterproof glue
String as needed
80–120-grit abrasive paper

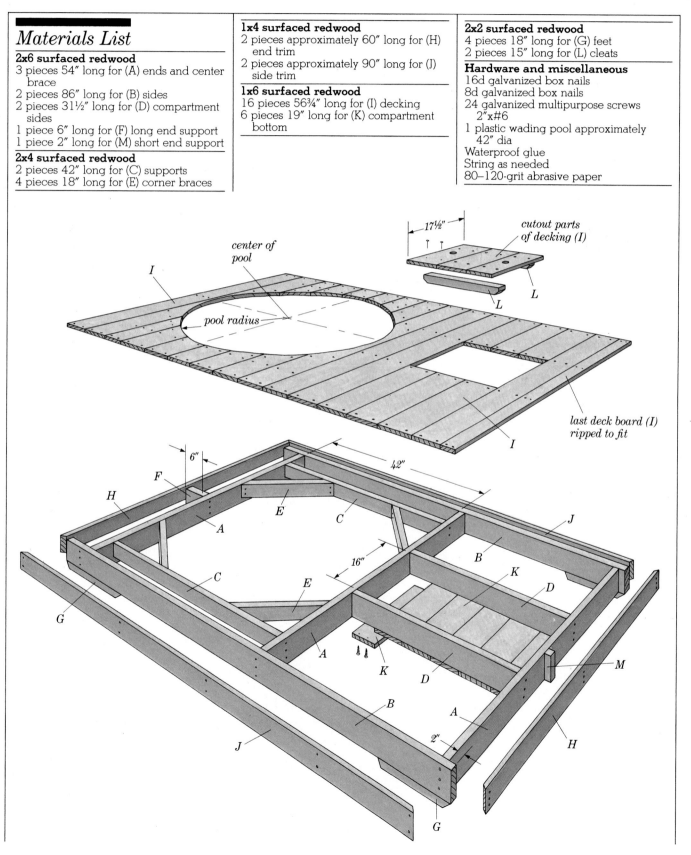

center of pool

pool radius

cutout parts of decking (I)

17½"

I

L

L

last deck board (I) ripped to fit

I

6"

F

H

A

E

C

C

E

A

G

42"

16"

B

K

D

J

K

D

A

M

B

A

H

J

2"

G

G

89

Garden Shelves

These shelves let you place a garden anywhere—under a window for viewing from either side of the glass, on a patio, or attached to a fence or wall. Shelves can be attached to a wall with nails or hung from screw eyes.

The dimensions of these shelves can easily be changed to fit your pots or the materials you have on hand. Plot curves on brackets with a compass, tin can, jar lid, or any other round object. None of the shapes are critical, so design the shelves to suit yourself.

For durable shelves, use kiln-dried redwood or cedar and apply a sealer after assembly. Finish with stain or paint if desired. See page 8 for information on wood finishes.

Simple Shelf

1. Cut shelf (I) and bracket (J).

2. With a saber saw, cut a decorative scroll on front edge of bracket, and round front corners of shelf if desired. Then use waterproof glue and 16-penny (16d) galvanized box nails to attach shelf to bracket.

3. Smooth rough edges of shelf with abrasive paper. Install 2 large screw eyes at back of shelf and hook them over nails or screws driven into a wall or fence.

Bracket Shelf

1. Cut shelf (K) and brackets (L).

2. Cut a 6-inch-deep by 6-inch-long notch in each bracket. Then cut a decorative scroll on front edge of brackets. Cut one bracket first and use it as a template to mark the other.

3. Round front corners of shelf with a coping or saber saw, if desired. Then assemble shelf and brackets with waterproof glue and 8d galvanized box nails. Place brackets about 6 inches from ends of shelf. Smooth rough edges of shelf with abrasive paper. Drill a ¼-inch hole through each bracket about 1 inch from top for mounting screws.

Slatted Shelves

1. Begin construction of either shelf by cutting front, side, and back pieces to size. For small shelf, cut off corners at top of back. Use waterproof glue and 8-penny (8d) galvanized box nails to attach front to sides, then attach back.

2. Cut bottom pieces so they fit exactly, and glue and nail them in place with equal spaces in between. Nail them to front and back as well as sides to strengthen shelves.

3. The chain is optional for decoration or to keep shelf from sagging from the weight of heavy pots or exposure to the weather.

4. Hang shelf on a fence or wall with nails through holes in back, or attach screw eyes and hang shelf from nails or screws.

Clockwise from upper left.
Simple Shelf, Small Slatted Shelf, Large Slatted Shelf, Bracket Shelf.
All of these shelves are very simple, but add a decorative touch to garden or patio and make pots more visible and accessible. The designs can be modified to fit whatever space is available. Slatted shelf design provides good drainage.

Materials List

Simple Shelf

2x10 surfaced redwood
1 piece 15" long for (I) shelf

2x6 surfaced redwood
1 piece 9" long for (J) bracket

Hardware and miscellaneous
16d galvanized box nails
2 large screw eyes
2 nails or screws as needed, for hanging
Waterproof glue
80–120-grit abrasive paper

Bracket Shelf

1x10 surfaced redwood
1 piece 36" long for (K) shelf

2x8 surfaced redwood
2 pieces 11" long for (L) brackets

Hardware and miscellaneous
8d galvanized box nails
2 flat-head wood screws 3"x#8 (or as
   long as needed, for hanging)
Waterproof glue
80–120-grit abrasive paper

Small Slatted Shelf

1x3 surfaced redwood
1 piece 7" long for (C) front
2 pieces 7¾" long for (B) sides
3 pieces 7" long for (D) bottom

2x6 surfaced redwood
1 piece 10" long for (A) back

Hardware and miscellaneous
8d galvanized box nails
2 screw eyes (optional)
Waterproof glue

Large Slatted Shelf

1x2 surfaced redwood
1 piece 36" long for (G) front
2 pieces 6¾" long for (F) sides
4 pieces 36" long for (H) bottom

1x6 surfaced redwood
1 piece 34½" long for (E) back

Hardware and miscellaneous
8d galvanized box nails
3 screw eyes
Waterproof glue
Chain and 2 screw eyes (optional)

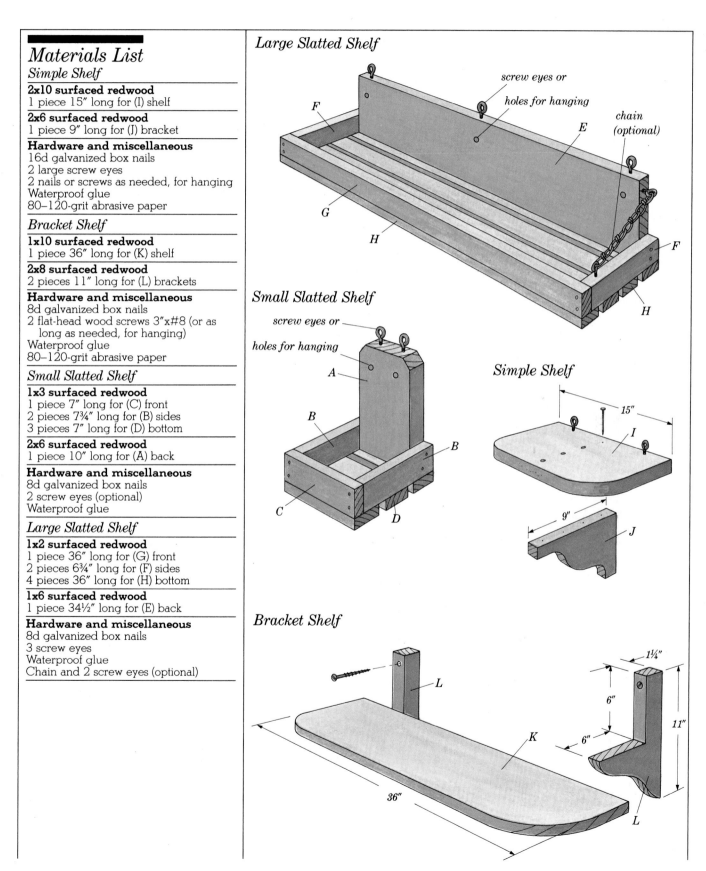

Large Slatted Shelf

Small Slatted Shelf

Simple Shelf

Bracket Shelf

A-frame Shelves

The attractive A-frame Shelves are sturdy yet light enough to carry. Use them to organize those stray clay pots, or make them the home for an herb garden. The shelves in the photograph measure 24 inches wide by 32 inches long, but the design can be altered to suit your needs.

1. Begin construction by cutting shelves (A), legs (B), upper braces (C), and lower braces (D).

2. Lay out and cut angles on top and bottom of legs according to the detail illustration. Position legs on upper braces and drill two ¼-inch holes through legs and braces for carriage bolts. Mark angle of legs on upper braces, then remove legs and cut braces to shape.

3. Assemble base by nailing shelves to lower braces with 8-penny (8d) galvanized box nails. Nail remaining shelf to upper braces. Then attach upper braces to legs with carriage bolts, washers, and nuts.

4. Position legs over base and drill ¼-inch holes for carriage bolts through legs and lower braces. Insert bolts and washers, and tighten nuts.

Materials List

1x8 surfaced redwood
5 pieces 24" long for (A) shelves

2x4 surfaced redwood
4 pieces 22" long for (B) legs
2 pieces 9" long for (C) upper braces
2 pieces 32" long for (D) lower braces

Hardware and miscellaneous
8d galvanized box nails
8 carriage bolts ¼"x3½", nuts, washers

Topped with a display of annuals, these A-frame Shelves provide a pyramid of color wherever your garden needs it.

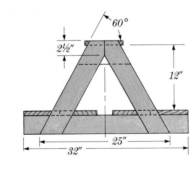

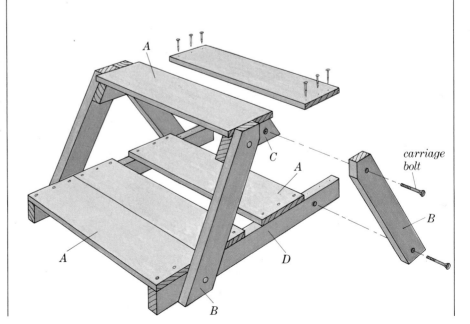

The materials listed make a 4-foot pedestal, but you can easily alter the lengths of the sides and corner pieces to make pedestals of varying heights.

1. Cut corner posts (A), crosspieces (B), sides (C), and top and base (D). Drill ½-inch or ¾-inch drainage holes in top and base.

2. Assemble frame first. Glue and nail corner posts to crosspieces with 8-penny (8d) galvanized box nails and waterproof glue. Place bottom crosspieces flush with bottom of posts, top pieces 8 inches from top, and center pieces halfway between the others.

3. Sides are ¼ inch larger than frame. Install first side so that one of its ends is flush with edge of frame. The other end protrudes ¼ inch. Use 3d galvanized box nails and glue. Attach next side flush against protruding surface of side you just installed. Attach other 2 sides in the same way.

4. Glue and nail base in place with 3d nails. Cut a 1½-inch-square notch in each corner of top so it drops down and rests on top crosspieces.

5. If desired, paint pedestal with exterior paint.

This display pedestal can be used indoors or outside. Make several of varying heights for a corner arrangement.

Materials List

2x2 surfaced redwood
4 pieces 48" long for (A) corner posts
12 pieces 10" long for (B) crosspieces

¼-inch exterior-grade plywood
4 pieces 13¼"x48" for (C) sides
2 pieces 13"x13" for (D) top and base

Hardware and miscellaneous
8d galvanized box nails
3d galvanized box nails
Waterproof glue
Exterior paint (optional)

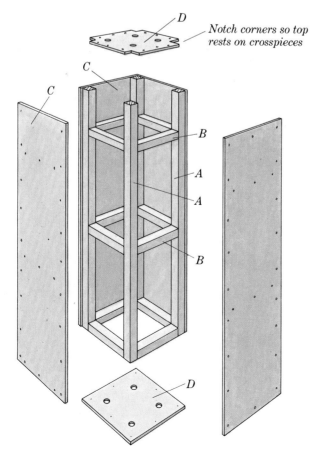

D — Notch corners so top rests on crosspieces

C
C
B
A
A
B
D

C *A* *C*

Sides (C) are cut ¼" wider than frame so corners of plywood overlap

U.S. Measure and Metric Measure Conversion Chart

		Formulas for Exact Measures			Rounded Measures for Quick Reference		
	Symbol	When you know:	Multiply by:	To find:			
Mass	oz	ounces	28.35	grams	1 oz		= 30 g
(Weight)	lb	pounds	0.45	kilograms	4 oz		= 115 g
	g	grams	0.035	ounces	8 oz		= 225 g
	kg	kilograms	2.2	pounds	16 oz	= 1 lb	= 450 g
					32 oz	= 2 lb	= 900 g
					36 oz	= 2¼ lb	= 1000g (1 kg)
Volume	tsp	teaspoons	5.0	milliliters	¼ tsp	= $^1/_{24}$ oz	= 1 ml
	tbsp	tablespoons	15.0	milliliters	½ tsp	= $^1/_{12}$ oz	= 2 ml
	fl oz	fluid ounces	29.57	milliliters	1 tsp	= ⅙ oz	= 5 ml
	c	cups	0.24	liters	1 tbsp	= ½ oz	= 15 ml
	pt	pints	0.47	liters	1 c	= 8 oz	= 250 ml
	qt	quarts	0.95	liters	2 c (1 pt)	= 16 oz	= 500 ml
	gal	gallons	3.785	liters	4 c (1 qt)	= 32 oz	= 1 liter
	ml	milliliters	0.034	fluid ounces	4 qt (1 gal)	= 128 oz	= 3¾ liter
Length	in.	inches	2.54	centimeters	⅜ in.	= 1 cm	
	ft	feet	30.48	centimeters	1 in.	= 2.5 cm	
	yd	yards	0.9144	meters	2 in.	= 5 cm	
	mi	miles	1.609	kilometers	2½ in.	= 6.5 cm	
	km	kilometers	0.621	miles	12 in. (1 ft)	= 30 cm	
	m	meters	1.094	yards	1 yd	= 90 cm	
	cm	centimeters	0.39	inches	100 ft	= 30 m	
					1 mi	= 1.6 km	
Temperature	°F	Fahrenheit	⅝ (after subtracting 32)	Celsius	32°F	= 0°C	
					68°F	= 20°C	
	°C	Celsius	$^9/_5$ (then add 32)	Fahrenheit	212°F	= 100°C	
Area	in.²	square inches	6.452	square centimeters	1 in.²	= 6.5 cm²	
	ft²	square feet	929.0	square centimeters	1 ft²	= 930 cm²	
	yd²	square yards	8361.0	square centimeters	1 yd²	= 8360 cm²	
	a.	acres	0.4047	hectares	1 a.	= 4050 m²	

INDEX